KARL MARX AND THE
CRITICAL EXAMINATION OF HIS WORKS

LESLIE R. PAGE

THE FREEDOM ASSOCIATION

LONDON

1987

First published in Great Britain, January 1987

British Library Cataloguing in Publication Data

Page, Leslie R.
   Karl Marx and the critical examination of his works.
   1. Marx, Karl, *1818-1883*
   i. Title ii. Freedom Association
   335.4'092'4   HX39.5

ISBN 1-870116-00-3

Printed by Reprocopy,
40 New Bridge Street, London EC4V 6BE.

Ruined! Ruined! My time has clean run out!
The clock has stopped, the pygmy house has crumbled,
Soon I shall embrace Eternity to my breast, and soon
I shall howl gigantic curses on mankind. ...

Ourselves being clockwork, blindly mechanical,
Made to be the fool-calendars of Time and Space,
Having no purpose save to happen, to be ruined,
So that there shall be something to ruin. ...

Ha, I must bind myself to a wheel of flame
And dance with joy in the circle of eternity!
If there is a Something which devours,
I'll leap within it, though I bring the world to ruins -
The world which bulks between me and the Abyss
I will smash to pieces with my enduring curses. ...

We are chained, shattered, empty, frightened,
Eternally chained to this marble block of Being,
Chained, eternally chained, eternally.
And the worlds drag us with them in their rounds,
Howling their songs of death, and we -
We are the apes of a cold God. ...

Oulanem, A Tragedy.

(*The Unknown Karl Marx,* edited and introduced
by Robert Payne, London, 1972, pp 81-83).

4

CONTENTS

NOTE All emphases in quotations are in the originals
unless otherwise stated.

ERRATA

Page 5 line 7: For "Third edition, 1986." read "Third edition, 1987."
Page 7 line 28: For "Novmber" read "November"
Page 120 line 27: For "*Das Kaptial*" read "*Das Kapital*"
Page 126 line 18: For "the fact that that" read "the fact that"
Page 141 Note 35: For "pp. 102, 103." read "pp. 101,102."

"The Red Prussian"

Leopold Schwarzschild's book *The Red Prussian: The Life and Legend of Karl Marx* was published in the United States in 1947 and in Great Britain in 1948. It has recently (1986) been reprinted by Pickwick Books Limited. The book is written with great verve and style and, despite omissions, it provides a well documented, critical account of Marx's life and work and fulfils a useful and important function. As Professor Settembrini, a former member of the Italian Communist Party, points out in Part Two of *Marxian Utopia?* (1985), a theoretical and historical critique of Marxism is indispensable for the comprehension of its influence and fate. One of the strengths of Schwarzschild's critical biography is that among its most frequently quoted sources is the collected edition of the works and correspondence of Marx and Engels issued by the Marx-Engels Institute in Moscow and published (1927-1935) in the original Gesamt - Ausgabe (= *MEGA*) edited by D. Rjazanov (later V. Adoratsky). Rjazanov 'disappeared' during the Soviet purges and the original *MEGA* was left unfinished. Schwarzschild claims that his book "makes no assertion, relates no episode, and emphasizes no trait in Marx's character without clinching the point by means of authentic quotations, and informing the reader where these quotations may be verified."

Since Schwarzschild's book was published, a second (East German) edition of the Marx-Engels Gesamtausgabe (henceforth *New MEGA*) was begun in 1975. There is also, in German, the (East Berlin) *Werke* (1956-1968), and the English language *Collected Works* (London and New York) begun in 1975. But, says Allen Oakley, in his book *The Making of Marx's Critical Theory,* 1983, p.ix, "There is still no *complete* edition of *all* of his [Marx's] extant works and no prospect of one. ... For example, the English edition of the *Collected Works* of Marx and Engels presently being published omits virtually all the notebook materials relating to Marx's studies of political economy during 1844-5 and 1851-3!" And according to David Felix, "Rjazanov was guided, as his successors have not been, by rigorous scholarly standards, and the *MEGA* includes a few items the *Werke* has not and the *New MEGA* has not yet published".(1) The *Collected Works,* the *Werke* and *New MEGA* do, however, contain extremely useful material which, in general, only reinforces the main thrust of Schwarzschild's work.

In the past forty years or so there has been a spate of writings on Marx and Marxism as more and more academics, propagandists, and publishers have sought to jump on the bandwagon, make money, further their careers, or promote their particular political ideology. Ill-informed, censored or falsified accounts of the ideas and influence of Karl Marx abound and fill the bookshops, but the hard-thinking and relevant, critical work seems to be known to comparatively few. How many Marxists, I wonder, are acquainted with the repeated racialistic utterances of Marx and Engels, or their justification of conquest, colonialism and the "supreme judgment" of war? How many are aware that Marx advocated child labour, or have studied the "plan of war against democracy" which Marx and Engels drew up together? How many know, say, H.W.B. Joseph's *The Labour Theory of Value in Karl Marx,* or Mark Blaug's *A Methodological Appraisal of Marxian Economics?* Are we to accept Ralph Miliband's assertion - in an article attacking Leszek Kolakowski's *Main Currents of Marxism* (3 volumes, 1978) - that "Marx was not, in fact, a 'German philosopher' ... No 'philosopher' of the kind Kolakowski has in mind could have written *Capital,* or would have felt any need to write it"? (2) Should we believe Tony Benn's claim that "unlike many philosophers ... Marx began by a deep study of the real world itself - in order to understand how it worked and why, and then drew his own conclusions"? (3)

The Shadow of Hegel

As Schwarzschild shows, Marx's first preoccupations were with poetry and philosophy and he became a communist largely under the influence of German philosophers. Engels in an article published in Novmber 1843 says that Marx had adopted "philosophical Communism". (4) And according to Allen Oakley, Marx's first known studies in political economy were recorded in a series of nine notebooks written early in 1844 in Paris. (5) Marx formed his viewpoint first and then went through whole libraries accumulating data and searching for proof of his pre-existing theory of communism. Martin Nicolaus writes of "the biographical fact that Marx proclaimed the historic liberating mission of the proletariat *before* he had more than the vaguest notions of the political economy of capitalism, before he had read the bourgeois economists of his day, ... ". (6) And as Angus Walker says: "Marx did not take up his economic studies, as we shall see later, simply to learn a new analytical technique; he did so to find support for ideas which he had already developed about the nature of social change." (7)

This is all brilliantly indicated by Schwarzschild - see pages 78, 82, 93, 107 and 110 of his book (1948 edition). Marx's *Capital,* said Henri Arvon, "is an authentic product of German philosophy". (8) "*Capital* itself begins and ends in metaphysics", says David Felix, "its economics doubled as Hegelian dialectics at all the hinge points. ... A half-hidden metaphysical structure holds the book together." (9) "Without German philosophy," declares Engels, "particularly that of Hegel, German scientific socialism would never have come into being". (10)

In a letter to Engels (14.1.1858) Marx, referring to his work on economics, wrote: "I am getting some nice developments. For instance, I have thrown over the whole doctrine of profit as it has existed up to now. In the method of treatment the fact that by mere accident I have again glanced through Hegel's *Logic* has been of great service to me." (11) Referring, in Volume 1 of *Capital,* to the minimum sum that the possessor of money or commodities must command in order to turn into a capitalist, Marx observes: "Here, as in natural science, is shown the correctness of the law discovered by Hegel (in his *Logic*), that merely quantitative differences beyond a certain point pass into qualitative changes". (12) "The whole of Part IV of Marx's *Capital, "* says Engels, deals "with innumerable cases in which quantitative change alters the quality, and also qualitative change alters the quantity." (13) In a letter to Conrad Schmidt on 1 November 1891, Engels writes: "It is impossible, of course, to dispense with Hegel ... . If you just compare the development of the commodity into capital in Marx with the development from Being to Essence in Hegel, you will get quite a good parallel for the concrete development which results from facts." (14) In an aphorism in his *Philosophical Notebooks* Lenin declared: "It is impossible completely to understand Marx's *Capital,* and especially its first chapter, without having thoroughly studied and understood the *whole* of Hegel's *Logic.*" (15)

Marx's Use of Dialectic

In *Letters to Dr. Kugelmann* (March 6, 1868 and June 27, 1870; 1941, pp. 63, 111) Marx writes: "Hegel's dialectic is the basic form of all dialectic, but only after it has been stripped of its mystical form, and it is precisely this which distinguishes my method. ... he [F.A. Lange] understands nothing about Hegel's method and secondly, as a consequence, even less about my critical application of it."

Marx's letter to Joseph Weydemeyer of 5 March, 1852 and his *Theories of Surplus Value* (1862-3, Part II, [Chap. IX], Section [2) reveal how he used a "critical application" of the dialectic of Hegel to project a view of history in which individuals and whole classes are sacrificed in a process which, Marx declares, will "necessarily" lead humanity to a classless, communist society: a society in which "the development of the capacities of the human species ... coincides with the development of the individual". (See p.126, and p.140 (Notes 28 and 29), of my *Marx and Darwin* (first published June 1983) reprinted as Appendix II to the present volume).

In a letter to Engels dated 15 August, 1857 - see pages 123-24 of *Marx and Darwin* (at Appendix II) - Marx also explains that "with the help of a bit of dialectics" one can always get out of a difficulty and formulate a proposition in such a way that no matter how events turn out it is possible to claim that it has been validated.

Volume 40 of the Marx-Engels *Collected Works,* which has now been published, includes this letter in which (see p. 152) Marx informs Engels that: "Being obliged for the present to hold the fort for you as the *Tribune's* military correspondent, I have taken it upon myself to put this forward. NB. on the supposition [in English] that the Reports [in English] to date have been true. It's possible that I shall make an ass of myself. But in that case one can always get out of it with a little dialectic. I have, of course, so worded my proposition as to be right either way."

In fact, in this instance - as in others - the historical events in question turned out quite differently to what Marx had really thought would happen. (See Marx-Engels, *Collected Works,* Vol. 40, p. 602, Note 186).

"Marx's dialectics", says Murray Wolfson, "permit him to avoid falsification because each assertion contains not only a thesis but an antithesis. Contradiction is part of the event. This is a very strange sort of logic, for if hypotheses are not falsifiable we dismiss them as meaningless and if they are contradicted by events we dismiss them as false. Marx's concept of science however included a new logic derived from Hegel's dialectical universal philosophy. ... But whatever the calculus - dialectic or otherwise - if it fails to put itself to the test by the device of absorbing self-contradiction into its system, it also absorbs the admission of its uselessness. ... at critical points in his argument when Marx is driven to contradiction between his analysis and the facts, he uses the dialectic to avoid the falsification to which his system would otherwise be subject." *(A Reappraisal of Marxian Economics,* 1966, p. 24).

"Alienation" and "Ideology"

The publication (in an incomplete Russian translation in 1927, complete in German in the original *MEGA* in 1932, and in English in 1959) of Marx's *Economic and Philosophical Manuscripts of 1844* aroused interest in the concept of "alienation" or "estrangement" and drew attention to Hegel's discussion of alienation in his *Phenomenology of Spirit* (1807). Marx was heavily influenced by Hegel and by Ludwig Feuerbach when he wrote his early manuscripts in 1844 but, says Richard Schacht, the centrality of the term *Entfremdung* in the *Manuscripts* "quite clearly derives from Hegel rather than from Feuerbach." (*Alienation,* 1972, p. 69).

Schacht's book and Walter Kaufmann's Introductory Essay entitled "The Inevitability of Alienation" are of great interest. Section 1 of Professor Kaufmann's essay provides an "Historical Perspective", Section 2 deals with "Alienated Philosophers", and Section 5 with "Marx's Dream." Section 7 which is headed "Against Marx's Heritage" includes a discussion of Marx's manuscript "Alienated Labour" and the birth of "the fateful Marxian idea that the condition of the workers is bound to become more and more inhuman and intolerable until there is a violent revolution in which, according to *Das Kapital,* 'the expropriators are expropriated' ".

In a passage from Marx's manuscript dealing with alienated labour Marx writes: "(The laws of political economy express the estrangement of the worker in his object thus: the more the worker produces, the less he has to consume; the more values he creates, the more valueless, the more unworthy he becomes; the better formed his product, the more deformed becomes the worker ; the more civilized his object, the more barbarous becomes the worker; the mightier labour becomes, the more powerless becomes the worker; the more ingenious labour becomes, the duller becomes the worker and the more he becomes nature's bondsman)." (*Manuscripts of 1844*, 1959, p. 71). But, as indicated by Kaufmann and pointed out in a more recent work by Richard Maycock, because the worker is legally separated or "alienated" from the product of his work, it does not follow that he must be "alienated" in the sense of being the victim of "impoverishment, degradation, dehumanization, barbarization, enfeeblement, and moronization." As Maycock says: "Like others of Marx's theories the doctrine [of alienation] rests on a non sequitur. It is a play on words." (*Alienation*, pp. xlix - 1 ; Richard Maycock, *Break The Deadlock*, Halifax, The Heigham Press, 1982).

Some of the ways in which Marx used "alienation", says Kaufmann, are "extremely far-fetched and should be given up." Kaufmann observes that Hegel had used the word "necessary" again and again in a confusing way and "among later German writers this confusion is common, and Marx's thought suffers severely from it." In the *1844 Manuscripts* (1959, pp. 68, 101-2) Marx writes of "a necessary course of development" and asserts that "communism already knows itself to be ... the transcendence of human self-estrangement; ... Communism is the riddle of history solved, and it knows itself to be this solution." In the Introduction to a dictionary of Marxism first published in the United States and Canada in 1986 it is asserted that communism will abolish the division of labor, seen by Marx and Engels as the first cause of social tyranny, and will mean that our modern technology will produce personal fulfilment and social justice. (*Biographical Dictionary of Marxism*, Edited by Robert A. Gorman, 1986, p.7).

An article on "alienation" in *A Dictionary of Marxist Thought* (1985), however, refers to a number of problems and controversial points concerning alienation and de-alienation. In one view described at some length on pages 14-15 "an individual can become a non-alienated, free and creative being only through his own activity." The problem of de-alienation of economic life "cannot be solved by the mere abolition of private property" or even by "the abolition of state property" and "its transformation into real social property" and "organizing the whole of social life on the basis of the self-management of the immediate producers. ... Some forms of alienation in production have their roots in the nature of present-day means of production, so that they cannot be eliminated by a mere change in the form of managing production."

Marx, says Schacht, gives the term "alienation" many different applications and the things he terms "alienated" differ considerably. In his hands the term becomes "little more than a general term whose utility lies primarily in the initial specification of a certain syndrome of separations, rather than in their closer analysis." Marx says, for instance, that: "In fact, the proposition that man's species nature is estranged from him means that one man is estranged from the other, as each of them is from man's essential nature." In another manuscript he asserts that: "Estrangement is manifested ... also in the fact that everything is in itself something *different* from itself - ... ." Marx's unrestricted usage, as Schacht's critical survey shows, set a precedent for later writers and seems to have inspired some "like Erich Fromm to refer to virtually *anything* which is not as it should be as an instance of 'alienation', regardless of whether the problems involved are in any way related." Kaufmann suggests that "alienation" has become a "bargain word" that costs "little or no study and can be used in a great variety of contexts with an air of expertise." Schacht's analysis demonstrates that it is now so loosely applied in connection with so many different phenomena that there is no "significant factual or conceptual connection between a great many of them" and the theory of alienation becomes, all too frequently, "a source of confusion and misunderstanding." (*Alienation,* pp. xlviii, 83, 113-14, 237-38; Marx, *Manuscripts of 1844,* 1959, pp. 77, 126).

One of the categories of Hegelian dialectical logic that shaped Marx's method in *Capital* and, says Jerrold Seigel, made many appearances in Marx's writings throughout his life, was the notion of inversion. (*Marx's Fate,* p. 357). In *The German Ideology* (1845-6) Marx and Engels write: "If in all ideology men and their relations appear upside-down as in a *camera obscura,* this phenomenon arises just as much from their historical life-process as the inversion of objects on the retina does from their physical life-process." (*Collected Works,* Vol. 5, p. 36). That is, says H.B. Acton in *The Illusion Of The Epoch,* "it is in the nature of things that men should get distorted views of the world, just as it is in the nature of things that they should receive inverted images on the retina."

In the same section in *The German Ideology,* Marx and Engels refer to "morality, religion, metaphysics, and all the rest of ideology" and contrast the "ideological reflexes" with "real, positive science" : "Where speculation ends, where real life starts, there consequently begins real, positive science, the expounding of the practical activity, of the practical process of development of men." (*Collected Works,* Vol. 5, pp. 36-7). And in the Preface to *A Contribution to the Critique of Political Economy* (1859), Marx distinguishes "the legal, political, religious, artistic or philosophic - in short, ideological forms" from "the material transformation of the economic conditions of production, which can be determined with the precision of natural science." (Peking, 1976, p.4). Thus, says Acton, the remarkable claims made for the Materialist Conception of History are that it "is not just another new view, but is the view which corrects and explains all other views, and differs from them in that, as scientific, it is not influenced by sectional prejudices." (H.B. Acton, *The Illusion Of The Epoch,* Second impression 1962, Part II, Chapter 1, Section 5, p. 179; see also pp. 172-73 and Section 2, pp. 126-28).

As Kenneth Minogue shows, however, in *Alien Powers : The Pure Theory of Ideology,* 1985 (p.2) : the term "ideology" was "coined during the French Revolution to describe a long-standing project of cognitive hygiene" but "it soon degenerated into a term of abuse meaning precisely what that project was designed to remedy. In this abusive form, it was taken up by Marx and Engels in the 1840's as a term for denigrating the competing thoughts of their fellow intellectuals." Marx criticized as ideology the illusions he believed himself to have found in "the ruling ideas of the epoch" but he "also believed that his science expressed the rising consciousness of the working class. Generalizing from this point, revolutionaries by the end of the century were using the word 'ideology' to mean any elaborated class point of view, all such viewpoints being partial and distorted except for that of the rising revolutionary class."

According to Bhikhu Parekh, Marx used the term "ideology" in several senses "to mean almost everything of which he disapproved. He used it to mean illusion (*German Ideology*), false ideas, any organised body of beliefs (*1859 Preface*), and even (*Theories of Surplus Value, 1975, Part I, pp. 285, 301)* the unproductive occupations." (*Marx's Theory of Ideology,* 1982, p. 230). It may be added that in Volume 1 of *Capital,* also, Marx writes of "the 'ideological' classes, such as government officials, priests, lawyers, soldiers, &c.." (Part IV, Chapter XV, Section 6., 1983, p.420).

An article on "ideology" in *A Dictionary of Marxist Thought* (1985) points out (p. 221) that the first thinker who posed the problem as to whether Marxism is an ideology was Eduard Bernstein and his answer "draws the obvious conclusion they [Mehring and Kautsky] had not drawn; namely, that Marxism must be an ideology." The article adds that none of Bernstein's Marxist critics "took him up on this issue," although he was already under attack for calling in question what he considered to be out-dated, dogmatic, unscientific or ambiguous elements in Marxism.

A number of important difficulties in Marx's conception of ideology and in his materialist conception of history are briefly considered in David McLellan's *Ideology* (Open University Press, 1986). The Introduction (p. xv) to *Politics and Ideology,* Edited by James Donald and Stuart Hall (Open University Press, 1986), refers to the 'base/superstructure' problem in the Marxian theory of ideology and to a debate as to what Marx 'really' intended. It also refers to another, equally contested, formulation by Marx in *The German Ideology* and says that he was working here at a very 'high' level of generalized abstraction and problems may have arisen because commentators attempted to interpret what is a very general statement in a literal way.

As Gordon Leff has pointed out, however, Marx took his notion of basis and superstructure as expressing social and historical reality. No one, says Leff, reading Marx from his early *Critique of Hegel's Philosophy of Right* to the final pages of *Capital* can doubt that his world of abstractions, 'proletariat', 'capital', 'class struggle', 'mode of production', stood directly for historical realities. He did not deny the reality of his categories, adds Leff, but rather hypostatized them as historical realities. He invested human history with the dialectical qualities that Hegel had applied to the unfolding of the absolute idea, so that Marx, no less than Hegel, saw in their operation the laws of historical development. The distinction between basis and super-structure, Leff concludes, is unreal and the materialist conception of history is inadequate to explain the motive force of change and in a number of other respects. (*The Tyranny of Concepts,* Second Edition, 1969, pp. 10, 149, 151).

In the view of Jorge Larrain, as stated in the last paragraph of an article on 'base and superstructure' in *A Dictionary of Marxist Thought* (1985, p. 45), ultimately the base-superstructure metaphor does not succeed in conveying a precise meaning. As A. James Gregor observed, twenty years previously, in his outstanding work, *A Survey of Marxism* (1965, pp. 183-4, 276-7, 281), apparently the wording of some of the "laws" or "tendencies" of historical materialism and their various formulations over a generation of literary activity, have left sufficient room for such varied opinions about their meaning that even specialists are confused as to their intent. If the "tendencies" governing a historical epoch are so vague that the proponents of the theory are in doubt concerning its specific implications it is difficult to understand under what conditions such a tendency is confirmed. In many cases theses are advanced which can neither be proved nor disproved because they are loosely framed and/or technical difficulties make them impossible to investigate. Engels's belief that "ultimately" economic "necessity" asserts itself, amid an "endless host of accidents", as the "determining element" in history, is one such example. Many of the "inevitabilities" of historical materialism operate in some such fashion : anything confirms the thesis, or confirmation is technically impossible, or confirmation can always be postponed to some future time.

In "A Short Digression on 'Ideology'" in *The Economics of Feasible Socialism* (1983, p. 116) Alec Nove suggests that we could, perhaps, best see ideology as colouring the spectacles through which reality is seen, or, changing the image, as a set of blinkers causing the wearer to reject certain solutions which might otherwise be possible.

"Man is not free to choose *his productive forces* upon which his whole history is based" or "this or that form of society", Marx told P.V. Annenkov in December 1846. (Marx-Engels, *Collected Works*, Vol. 38). And in the Preface of 1859 to *A Contribution to the Critique of Political Economy* (1981, p. 20), Marx states that "In the social production of their existence, men inevitably enter into definite relations, which are independent of their will, namely relations of production appropriate to [which correspond to] a given stage in the development of their material forces of production." A footnote in Volume 1 of Marx's *Capital* (Chapter 1, Section 4, 1983, p.86) refers to the *Critique of Political Economy* and to "my view that each special mode of production and the social relations corresponding to it, in short, that the economic structure of society, is the real basis on which the juridical and political superstructure is raised, and to which definite social forms of thought correspond; that the mode of production determines the character of the social, political, and intellectual life generally." In *Theories of Surplus Value* [Volume IV of *Capital*], Part I (1975, p.285), Marx writes: "from the specific form of material production arises in the first place a specific structure of society, in the second place a specific relation of men to nature. Their State and their spiritual outlook is determined (*bestimmt*) by both. Therefore also the kind of their spiritual production." And in the *Grundrisse* (Penguin Books, 1973, p. 88) Marx says that "every form of production creates its own legal relations, form of government, etc."

The "multiplied productive force, which arises through the co-operation of different individuals ... appears to these individuals," Marx and Engels tell us, "as an alien force existing outside them, of the origin and goal of which they are ignorant, which they thus are no longer able to control, which on the contrary passes through a peculiar series of phases and stages independent of the will and the action of man, nay even being the prime governor of these." (*The German Ideology, Collected Works*, Vol. 5, p. 48). G.A. Cohen, who quotes this passage (in *Karl Marx's Theory of History: A Defence*, 1979, p. 148), admits that that there is a sense in which the productive forces may dominate the men whose forces they are, and that Marx says so. Cohen adds that history is the development of human productive power but the course of its development is not subject to human will. It is "an old-fashioned historical materialism", "a traditional conception", which Cohen says (p. x) he defends. But in a systematic criticism in *New Left Review* (Sept.-Oct. 1980) Andrew Levine and Erik Olin Wright conclude that "the 'orthodoxy' Cohen has reconstructed and defended" is "ultimately inadequate politically as well as theoretically, whatever its roots in Marx's writings."

Marx's claims are rejected in Karl Federn's critical analysis *The Materialist Conception of History* (1939 and 1971) which, although it was written almost 50 years ago, is a powerful and lucid refutation, based on insights and arguments which have been taken up by later writers. Federn's book is not included in the Bibliography in David McLellan's *Karl Marx: His Life and Thought* (1973) or, for example, in the works cited in G.A. Cohen's *Karl Marx's Theory of History* (1979). Federn starts from what is called the "classical formulation" of the materialist conception of history, the propositions put forward by Karl Marx in the *1859 Preface* which Federn considers along with other writings on the subject.

The productive forces, says Federn, do not play the part in history that Marx and his followers ascribe to them. Marx neglected to investigate how the development and increasing command of the productive forces is brought about. The productive forces are discovered, developed and applied by the human intellect, by human insight and will-power. All Marx's speculation is fatally vitiated by his fundamental mistake, which is to discard intellect in history as much as possible. Whereas Marx asserts in the *Preface* that "It is not the consciousness of men that determines (*bestimmt*) their existence, but their social existence that determines their consciousness," it does not seem possible to conceive of any social relation independently of forms of consciousness.

As Federn points out, Marx did not merely wish to imply that society depends on production for its existence. This is a truism and no one, in this case, would have contested his theory. What Marx wanted to say was not only that production is necessary, but that the mode of production and the corresponding social relations are decisive and when the mode of production changes, everything else changes. In Marx's theory, a number of phenomena are segregated from the infinite connection of events and declared to be basic; or they are said by Engels to be the "most decisive" or ultimately the "determining (*bestimmende*) element" or "the determining basis of the history of society." (Marx-Engels, *Selected Correspondence,* 1941, pp. 475, 484, 516). No one, however, says Federn, has yet been able to furnish the necessary proofs. Is it possible to believe for a moment that government, armies, as instruments of politics, wars, religion and laws, intellectual development and opinions should have so much less influence on economic conditions than agriculture, manufacture and wages have on the former? And how could one divide the countless interacting economic and non-economic factors and say which played the larger role? (Federn, op. cit., Chapter III; Peter Singer, *Marx,* 1980, p. 40).

Referring to Federn's criticism, William H. Shaw says that "human knowledge and productive intelligence are already built into Marx's conception of the productive forces". (*Marx's Theory of History*, 1978, p. 65). As Federn points out, however, the development of the productive forces "implies a certain inter-connection and inter-dependency between economic necessities, the human mind and production. ... The whole matter takes on a different aspect if we decide to rate the human mind among the productive forces. ... Neither Marx himself nor his followers seem ever to have made a thorough study of this question." In a critical analysis of Marx's theory Federn shows that "no one can say which of these inter-dependent elements is the first or primary agency" and the distinction between basis and superstructure is "purely theoretical, possible only in words", and does not correspond to reality. (op. cit., pp. 14, 17-18, 153-4). In *The Political Economy Of Marx* (Second edition, 1985, Chapter 1), M.C. Howard and J.E. King say that Engels's reformulation of the materialist conception of history is of exactly the same non-scientific status as Marx's.

Writing 35 years after Federn, the New Left author, Perry Anderson, concludes, in the closing section of his *Lineages of the Absolutist State* (1974, Second Impression 1984, pp. 403-4), that: "In consequence, pre-capitalist modes of production cannot be defined *except* via their political, legal and ideological superstructures, ..." These modes of production "operate through *extra-economic* sanctions - kin, customary, religious, legal or political. It is therefore on principle always impossible to read them off from economic relations as such." Here, therefore, the distinction between base and superstructure collapses, together with Marx's theory of history.

In *The German Ideology* (Marx-Engels, *Collected Works*, Vol. 5, pp. 31, 36-7, 287) the "real life-process" of "real, active men" who "*produce* their means of subsistence" is contrasted with "the ideological reflexes and echoes of this life-process." The "phantoms formed in the brains of men" are said to be "necessarily, sublimates of their material life-process, which is empirically verifiable and bound to material premises." And, according to Marx and Engels, "ideal collisions" i.e. collisions between "individuals and the ideas which they form or get into their heads," are "the ideal reflection", the "ideal copy", of "real collisions" i.e. collisions between "individuals and their actual conditions of life." The conception being advanced here is that consciousness is a "sublimate", a "reflex" and "echo", an "ideal reflection" or "ideal copy" of the material life-process of men. "It is not consciousness that determines life, but life that determines consciousness." This is repeated in the *1859 Preface* (1981, p. 21).

For Marx, says Peter Singer, the productive life of human beings, rather than their ideas and consciousness, is ultimately real. (see pp. 41-43, *Marx*, 1980). And in *Karl Marx's Theory of History: A Defence* (1979, p. 137) G.A. Cohen admits that sentences in the *1859 Preface* "do assign a derivative role to social consciousness." Not only that, but again in 1873, in the Afterword to the second German edition of Volume 1 of *Capital* (1983, p. 29), Marx declares that: "With me, on the contrary, the ideal [the life-process of the human brain, i.e., the process of thinking,] is nothing else than the material world reflected by the human mind, and translated into forms of thought."

Consciousness, says Jorge Larrain, in *A Reconstruction of Historical Materialism,* 1986, p.18, is dealt with in the context of the base-superstructure metaphor as a passive reflection of material life. According to Larrain, Marx gives two conflicting accounts of consciousness, a tension derived from his attempt to integrate elements of philosophical materialism with the 'active side' developed by idealism. Cohen (op. cit., 1979, p. 248) points out that when critics of historical materialism claim that dimensions other than the mode of production are fundamental, it is no reply to insert those dimensions into the mode of production. Marx himself, it may be noted, in his main work, refers to the capitalist as "personified capital" and, to a considerable degree, the actions of a capitalist "are a mere function of capital - endowed as capital is, in his person, with consciousness and a will." (*Capital,* Vol. 1, Part VII, Chapter XXIV, Section 3, 1983, p.555).

Larrain's list of "References" includes Federn's book but not Paul Q. Hirst's *Marxism and Historical Writing,* 1985, which deals with G.A. Cohen's attempt to defend Marx's theory of history. Cohen's attempt, says Hirst (p.42), is on balance a failure, but it fails not in pursuing some eccentricity of Cohen's but a central proposition in Marxist discourse, that is, "the primacy of the 'forces of production' ".

In the Preface to the *Critique of Political Economy* (1981, p. 21)

Marx states that: "At a certain stage of development, the material productive forces of society come into conflict with the existing relations of production ... Then begins an era of social revolution. The changes in the economic foundation lead sooner or later to the transformation of the whole immense superstructure. In studying such transformations it is always necessary to distinguish between the material transformation of the economic conditions of production, which can be determined with the precision of natural science, and the legal, political, religious, artistic or philosophic - in short, ideological forms in which men become conscious of this conflict and fight it out. ... one cannot judge such a period of transformation by its consciousness, but, on the contrary, this consciousness must be explained from the contradictions of material life, from the conflict existing between the social forces of production and the relations of production."

Thus, says Gregor, it is only when the material productive forces can no longer freely develop within the confines of the existing production and property relations that social revolution begins. Revolution, by virtue of which historical change occurs is precipitated by changes in the productive forces. "Capitalist production", declares Marx in Volume 1 of *Capital,* "begets with the inexorability of a law of nature its own negation. It is the negation of negation." (Chapter XXXII, 1983, p. 715).

After having in an arbitrary way constructed the history of the past, says Federn, Marx feels equal to the task of delineating the history of the future. In the *1859 Preface* Marx announces that: "In broad outlines, Asiatic, ancient, feudal and modern bourgeois modes of production can be designated as progressive epochs in the economic formation of society." He then goes on to say that: "The bourgeois relations of production are the last antagonistic form of the social process of production - antagonistic not in the sense of individual antagonism, but of one arising from the social conditions of life of the individuals; at the same time the productive forces developing in the womb of bourgeois society create the material conditions for the solution of that antagonism. This social formation brings, therefore, the prehistory of human society to a close." (As cited at the front of G.A. Cohen's book, *Karl Marx's Theory of History:A Defence,* 1979).

The antagonism resulting from the social conditions of the individuals, Federn says, is class war, of which there has been no question in the *1859 Preface* until now; it is, however, sufficiently discussed in Marx's other writings. This antagonism, this class war, is to cease completely after the coming revolution. The new productive forces growing in the womb of existing society will make this possible. Marx introduces his judgments in the disguise of a pretended law that is to bring about of necessity that state which he considers just and desirable. But this has nothing to do with history. "It is of no use to oppose scientific arguments to a man who is conscious of understanding the present and of seeing the future."

The materialist conception of history, says Peter Singer, was conceived as an explanation of history as a necessary process heading towards a discoverable goal. (*Marx,* 1980, pp. 42-3). In an article on "The British Rule in India" (1853) Marx referred to "mankind's destiny" and to England as "the unconscious tool of history." And in a letter to Joseph Weydemeyer (5 March, 1852) he pretended to have shown that the class struggle "necessarily" leads to the revolutionary "*dictatorship of the proletariat*" and a "*classless society.*" (Marx-Engels, *Collected Works,* Vol.12, p. 132; Vol. 39, pp. 62, 65).

In *Karl Marx's Theory of History: A Defence* (1979, p. 147, footnote 1), G.A. Cohen says that "the issue of determinism will not be discussed in this book;" he discusses "functional explanation," in general and with greater reference to historical materialism. According to an article by Gregor McLennan in the Spring, 1986 issue of *Science & Society,* however, Cohen "has now admitted difficulties with his theory of history" and "is no longer sure whether historical materialism is true." ("Marxist Theory and Historical Research : Between the Hard and Soft Options").

Chapters IV to VII of Karl Federn's book deal with "The Great Social Revolutions", "The Historical Epochs According to Marx", "Historical Dialectics", and "The Doctrine Of Necessity According To Marx". At the end of Chapter VII Federn claims that Marx's description of the great social revolutions and his classification of historical periods has been shown to be erroneous, and it has been demonstrated that his dialectics and doctrines of historical necessity are vague, founded on a delusion produced by mere words and on a false idea of real historical developments. In no way is Marx's theory of history sufficient to explain historical events and their causation.

Marx's attempt, in his Introduction of 1857 to the *Grundrisse,* to explain the continuing aesthetic appeal of Greek art in terms of the "eternal charm" exercised by the historical childhood of humanity, is described by Raymond Williams, in an essay on "Culture" published in 1983, as "absurd". (*Marx: The First 100 Years,* edited by David McLellan, 1983, p. 46). The inadequacy of Marx's theory was pointed out long ago, for example, by M.M. Bober (in *Karl Marx's Interpretation of History,* Chapter XVIII) and by Peter Demetz (in *Marx, Engels, and the Poets: Origins of Marxist Literary Criticism,* English edition, 1967, pp. 67-73; German edition, Stuttgart, 1959). Just at the point where Marx was willing "to apply his theory to a concrete phenomenon of art", says Demetz, "the theory proves to be completely incapable of encompassing the reality;" and in the Preface to the *Critique of Political Economy* "the role of the creative human being appeared reduced to an all but absurd level."

In historical materialism, the resolution of disputed claims to right and of ideological conflict is left, says Timothy McCarthy, "to the ultimate arbiter: force and might." (*Marx and the Proletariat,* 1978, pp. 50-51). As Marx puts it in Volume 1 of *Capital:* "There is here, therefore, an antimony, right against right, both equally bearing the seal of the law of exchanges. Between equal rights force decides." (Chap. X, Section 1., 1983, p. 225). And in *The German Ideology* Marx and Engels write: "Both for the production on a mass scale of this communist consciousness, and for the success of the cause itself, the alteration of men on a mass scale is necessary, an alteration which can only take place in a practical movement, a *revolution* ; the revolution is necessary, therefore, not only because the *ruling* class cannot be overthrown in any other way, but also because the class *overthrowing* it can only in a revolution succeed in ridding itself of all the muck of ages and become fitted to found society anew." (*Collected Works,* Vol. 5, pp. 52-3).

As Bruce Mazlish remarks in *The Meaning of Karl Marx* (1984, p. 168), Marx's revolutionary desires, which require a communist revolution, and the millenial aspirations of Marxism, can readily lead to undesirable totalistic ends. "The trails that ideologists have blazed", says Lewis S. Feuer, "have led to the fires of the Nazi crematoria, and to the Arctic wastes of the Soviet labour camps." (*Ideology And The Ideologists,* 1975, p. 191).

The False Flag

Chapter 10 of Schwarzschild's book shows how Marx and Engels, after becoming members of the Communist League and publishing the *Manifesto of the Communist Party* (February, 1848) and the *Demands of the Communist Party in Germany* (March, 1848), adopted the strategy of "the false flag", keeping the communist flag out of sight and unfurling the more magnetic banner of democracy. The *Communist Manifesto* and the *Communist Demands* had had little influence and as Engels later admitted Marx and he "joined the Democratic Party as the only possible means of getting the ear of the working class". Marx became Editor-in-Chief of the *New Rhenish Gazette* of Cologne the first number of which was dated June 1, 1848. Described by the Marx-Engels-Lenin Institute in Moscow as "the first Marxist newspaper" it bore the misleading subtitle "Organ of Democracy". It was not a democratic organ but a communist one. It was run entirely by communists - formerly members of the Communist League - and Marx wielded absolute power over what went into the paper. As stated in an article written by Engels, who was one of the editors, "The editorial constitution was simply the dictatorship of Marx". (16).

An article in the *New Rhenish Gazette* (17.9.1848) on "Freedom of Debate in Berlin", written by Marx or Engels or jointly by them, declares: " 'Freedom of Debate' - there is no emptier phrase than this. The 'freedom of debate' is, on the one hand, impaired by the freedom of the press, by the freedom of assembly and of speech, and by the right of the people to take up arms". (17). In *The German Ideology* (1845-6) Marx and Engels wrote: "As far as law is concerned, we with many others have stressed the opposition of communism to law, both political and private, as also in its most general form as the rights of man". (18) And when Marx was being tried for publishing insulting remarks in the *New Rhenish Gazette* he told the jury (7.2.1849) that "The first duty of the press, therefore, is to undermine all the foundations of the existing political system". (19)

"Force is the Midwife "

According to Marx (*New Rhenish Gazette*, 7.11.1848) "there is only *one means* by which the murderous death agonies of the old society and the bloody birth throes of the new society can be *shortened,* simplified and concentrated - and that is by *revolutionary terror".* (20) And as stated by Engels in 1873: "A revolution is certainly the most authoritarian thing there is; it is the act whereby one part of the population imposes its will upon the other part by means of rifles, bayonets and cannon ... and if the victorious party does not want to have fought in vain, it must maintain this rule by means of the terror which its arms inspire in the reactionaries." (21) "Force", says Marx in *Capital,* "is the midwife of every old society pregnant with a new one." (22)

In 1880-1881, thirteen years or so after the publication of *Capital* and two or three years before his death, Marx was in contact with L.N. Hartmann and N.A. Morozov, members of the Russian revolutionary populist group People's Will (*Narodnaya Volya*), in whose terrorist activities Hartmann played a key role. Following the assassination of Alexander II by the Narodnaya Volya in March 1881, Marx (in a letter to his daughter Jenny dated 11 April 1881) described the terrorists as "sterling people through and through, with no melo-dramatic pose, simple, businesslike, heroic. ... far removed from the schoolboy way in which Most and other childish whimperers preach tyrannicide as a 'theory' and 'panacea'." The People's Will, said Marx, "try to teach Europe that their mode of operation is a specifically Russian and historically inevitable method about which there is no more reason to moralise - for or against - than there is about the earthquake in Chios" [this referred to a recent earthquake in Greece]. "Marx", says David McLellan (*Karl Marx,* 1973, p. 441), "had much less respect for the populist exiles in Geneva (among them Plekhanov and Axelrod) who were opposed to terrorism and preferred to concentrate on propaganda." (See also *Late Marx and the Russian Road,* edited by Teodor Shanin, 1983, pp. 61, 166, 173-74, 275; Marx-Engels, *Selected Correspondence,* 1941, pp. 390-91).

According to the *Communist Manifesto:* "National differences and antagonisms between peoples are daily more and more vanishing", and "United action, of the leading civilised countries at least, is one of the first conditions for the emancipation of the proletariat". (23) Yet, as Schwarzschild shows, only a few months after the *Manifesto* was published, Marx and Engels "blew the trumpet of war" believing that the adversaries of the masses would be "weakened through having their armies engaged in war".

In the *New Rhenish Gazette* they wrote of "a war of *revolutionary Germany* by which she could cleanse herself of her past sins, could take courage, defeat her own autocrats, spread civilisation by the sacrifice of her own sons ..." (12.7.1848); of a "general war" which will "wipe out all these petty, hidebound nations down to their very names".; of a "world war" which "will result in the disappearance from the face of the earth not only of reactionary classes and dynasties, but also of entire reactionary peoples. And that, too, is a step forward". (13.1.1849); of "hatred of Russia" which "was and still is the *primary revolutionary passion* among Germans" ... "hatred of Czechs and Croats" ... "and that only by the most determined use of terror against these Slav peoples can we, jointly with the Poles and Magyars, safeguard the revolution" (16.2.1849). (24)

Included in these writings was the contemptuous denunciation of "historyless peoples" (a notion, says Ian Cummins, originally derived from Hegel) and statements which, as Cummins puts it, smack "more of racism than of 'scientific socialism' ". (25) The *New Rhenish Gazette* also contained what David McLellan describes as "a fair amount of anti-semitism". (26) Many of these articles came from Müller-Tellering whose contributions, Marx said (in a letter of 5.12.1848), were "incontestably the best we receive, completely in line with our own tendency, ...". (27)

The *Grundrisse*

As Schwarzschild shows (op.cit., 1948, pp. 236-40), Marx was continually prophesying economic crises, catastrophe, and revolution. (see also McLellan, *Karl Marx*, 1973, pp. 281-82; Fred M. Gottheil, *Marx's economic predictions,* 1966, Chapter 12). In 1855, for example, referring to a demonstration in Hyde Park, Marx wrote that we "do not think we are exaggerating in saying that the English Revolution began yesterday in Hyde Park." (Marx-Engels, *On Religion,* Moscow, 1981, pp. 111-12). And in 1857-8 Marx declared: "these regularly recurring catastrophes lead to their repetition on a higher scale, and finally to its [capital's] violent overthrow." (*Grundrisse,* Penguin Books, 1973, p. 750).

In a letter to Lassalle (21 December, 1857) Marx told him that "The present commercial crisis has impelled me to set to work seriously on my outlines of political economy, and also to prepare something on the present crisis." And in a letter to Engels (8 December, 1857) Marx wrote: "I am working like mad all night and every night collating my economic studies so that I at least get the outlines [*Grundrisse*] clear before the *déluge."* (Marx-Engels, *Collected Works, Vol. 40,* 1983, pp. 226, 217). "Of course", says Roman Rosdolsky, Marx's "revolutionary prognosis was based on an illusion." (*The Making of Marx's 'Capital',* 1980, p.7).

The manuscripts which have become known as the *Grundrisse* ('Outlines' or 'Foundations') include a series of seven notebooks rough-drafted by Marx chiefly for purposes of self-clarification, and an Introduction, all written in 1857-58. The manuscripts were first published in German in Moscow (1939 and 1941) and the title - translated as *Foundations of the Critique of Political Economy (Rough Draft)* - was chosen by the original editors. A. James Gregor makes some use of the Berlin, 1953, edition of the *Grundrisse* in his *A Survey of Marxism,* 1965.

When Marx was writing the *Grundrisse* he re-read Hegel's *Logic* and, as noted by Oakley (*The Making of Marx's Critical Theory,* 1983, pp. 62-3), in "The Chapter on Capital" (*Grundrisse,* pp. 275 ff.) Marx uses 'very Hegelian' terminology and "applies the logical triad of generality, particularity, and individuality directly to the analysis of the category of capital." And immediately following this he develops more fully "the *logic* of the capital - landed property - wage labour triad." As Jerrold Seigel remarks (*Marx's Fate,* p. 372) the publication of the *Grundrisse* - which makes up a large book of over 800 pages - contained many surprises for those scholars who did not know of Marx's return to Hegel in 1857.

The *Grundrisse* which, says Professor Hobsbawm, was composed by Marx in preparation for his *Contribution to the Critique of Political Economy* and *Capital,* is permeated with Hegelian language and as stated by Martin Nicolaus - who translated the *Grundrisse* - "the usefulness of Hegel" to Marx "lay in providing guide-lines for what to do... ." In the *Grundrisse* Marx repeatedly invokes Hegel, and refers, for example, to "alienation", to "negation of the negation" and "the suspension of this suspension", to "these opposites ... the suspension of these opposites", to "the general" as "at the same time a *particular* real form alongside the form of the particular and individual", and to "values" which "out of the form of unrest ... condense themselves into a resting, objective form, in the product."

Marx also writes about Adam Smith, Ricardo, and other economists, and about "abstract labour", "constant" and "variable" capital, "labour power", "necessary" and "surplus" labour, and "surplus value". And on the very last page of the *Grundrisse's* seventh notebook there is a section subtitled by Marx "(1) Value" with the note "This section to be brought forward". It begins: "The first category in which bourgeois wealth presents itself is that of the *commodity*. The commodity itself appears as unity of two aspects [i.e. use value and exchange value]". This conclusion forms the starting point of Marx's *Critique of Political Economy* and of Volume 1 of *Capital. Capital* opens with the words: "The wealth of those societies in which the capitalist mode of production prevails, presents itself as 'an immense accumulation of commodities', its unit being a single commodity. Our investigation must therefore begin with the analysis of a commodity". Thus, the *Grundrisse* manuscripts, profoundly influenced by Hegelian thought and mixing philosophy with economic theory, constitute a preliminary draft for Marx's mature economic writings and projected work on his 'Economics'.

On pp. 747 ff. of the *Grundrisse* Marx discusses the theory of the fall in the rate of profit as society progresses and says: "This is in every respect the most important law of modern political economy, ... The growing incompatibility between the productive development of society and its hitherto existing relations of production expresses itself in bitter contradictions, crises, spasms. The violent destruction of capital ... ." In *Marx's Fate* (Chap. Eleven) Jerrold Seigel draws attention to differences between the manuscripts left by Marx and the text Engels published for that part of *Capital* (Vol. III) devoted to "The Law of the Tendency of the Rate of Profit to Fall." Seigel concludes that Marx knew the law "could not be verified empirically and his commitment to it led him into a maze of argumentation so intricate that even he himself might sometimes lose his way in it."

A long article by Geoff Hodgson on "The Theory of the Falling Rate of Profit" (incorporating a survey of empirical data for the United States) evaluates the validity of Marx's theory - "regarded by most Marxists as the backbone of revolutionary Marxism." Hodgson's conclusion is that "we must bury the last iron law of Marxian economy - the law of the falling tendency of the rate of profit." (*New Left Review,* March-April 1974). Other critical surveys of this theory may be found, for example, in Mark Blaug's *A Methodological Appraisal of Marxian Economics* (1980, Lecture 2), in Jon Elster's *Making Sense of Marx* (1985), and in the second edition of *The Political Economy Of Marx* by M.C. Howard and J.E. King (1985). Howard and King declare their support for Marxian methods, broadly defined, but they conclude that, on Marx's assumptions, the occurrence of a falling rate of profit in the manner he suggested, is an impossibility. And in Chapter 10 (p. 171) of their book they say that the "solution" to the Marxian "transformation problem" [the procedure for 'transforming' surplus value into profit and values into prices of production] outlined in their Chapter 8 is no longer valid, now that further considerations have been taken into account, even in free competition.

When Marx published *A Contribution to the Critique of Political Economy* in 1859 he withheld the Introduction which he had drafted in 1857. He said that "on further consideration it seems to me confusing to anticipate results which still have to be substantiated, and the reader who really wishes to follow me will have to decide to advance from the particular to the general." (*Critique of Political Economy,* 1981, p. 19). As Seigel comments, the account which Marx gave in 1859 of his development hid as much as it revealed. The return to Hegel which the *Grundrisse* exhibited so richly was concealed. (op.cit., p. 372). Marx's general method of enquiry has been critically analysed and assessed by Seigel (see, in particular, chapters 10 and 12 of *Marx's Fate,* 1978) and by Blaug (*A Methodological Appraisal of Marxian Economics,* 1980, and other works). Neither of these authors, however, is included in the Bibliography or Notes to the Afterword in Derek Sayer's *Marx's Method* (Second edition, 1983). Sayer does say at one point that "Contrary to the *Grundrisse,* then, it *is* at some stage necessary to write 'the real history of the relations of production' if we are fully to understand the 'laws' of bourgeois economy." (op. cit., p. 159). This refers to Marx's assertion that "In order to develop the laws of bourgeios economy, therefore, it is not necessary to write the *real history of the relations of production."* (*Grundrisse,* 1973, p. 460).

In "Whatever Happened To The Labour Theory Of Value?" (in

Essays In Economic Analysis, 1976), the economist Ronald L. Meek, who was for many years a teacher of Marxist economics, considers Marx's procedure in Volume 1 of *Capital* in "starting with values" - these "mysterious, non-observable, volume 1 'values'." He goes on to assert that this procedure, although it assumed a logical form, had a significant 'historical' dimension i.e. there were correspondences between the course of Marx's logic and the course of history. Meek calls this "Marx's 'logical-historical method', one of the most interesting and significant fruits of his early Hegelian studies." (pp. 245-46, 253-54).

Meek admits that this runs the risk of getting the reply that this is no justification at all, since there never was in fact an identifiable historical period characterised by the fact that commodities sold at their 'values'. But, curiously enough, he thinks this would be a "misunderstanding, if not a trivialisation" although, at the same time, he acknowledges that Engels "went overboard a bit" in declaring that "simple commodity production" and the Marxian law of value "prevailed during a period of from five to seven thousand years." (pp. 254, 258).

In fact, as pointed out by Morishima and Catephores: "the opinion of Engels has been rejected by various subsequent Marxian authors" and "if the level of abstraction of a scheme is so high as to present a very selective conformity with historical reality, then ... it ... may risk taking us ... into the realm of almost purely logical exercise." (*Value, Exploitation and Growth,* 1978, pp. 180, 182). As Blaug puts it (op.cit., 1980, p. 20): "no one has ever discovered a single piece of evidence that would support the notion of the existence of a system of 'simple commodity production' lasting for centuries somewhere in Europe."

"Pre-Capitalist Modes of Production" and "Asiatic Despotism"

A part of "The Chapter on Capital" in the *Grundrisse* was translated into English and published separately in 1964 under the title *Pre-Capitalist Economic Formations* with an Introduction by the Marxist historian E.J. Hobsbawm. In *Were Marx and Engels White Racists?* (1972) Carlos Moore quotes this Introduction extensively. Hobsbawm, says Moore, has clarified a point which has never been sufficiently stressed. Moore refers to Marx's and Engels' ignorance or superficial knowledge of non-Western societies. He also draws attention to their Euro-centric orientation and racial attitudes.

"It is generally agreed," Hobsbawm writes, "that Marx and Engels' observations on pre-capitalist epochs rest on far less thorough study than Marx's descriptions and analysis of capitalism. ... So much for the general state of Marx's and Engels' historical knowledge. We may summarise it as follows. It was (at all events in the period when the *Formen* [*"Forms which precede capitalist production"* in the *Grundrisse*] were drafted) thin on pre-history, on primitive communal societies and on pre-Colombian America, and virtually non-existent on Africa. It was not impressive on the ancient or medieval Middle East, but markedly better on certain parts of Asia, notably India, but not on Japan. It was good on classical antiquity and the European Middle Ages ... ."

So far as India is concerned, Bipan Chandra's judgment, in "Karl Marx, His Theories of Asian Societies, and Colonial Rule" (1981), is that "Historical research over the last 100 years or so, including the recent work of Marxist scholars, has shown that Marx's basic notions regarding Indian society were essentially incorrect." Furthermore, "Marx's overall analysis of Asian societies and colonialism has proved to be inadequate and does not stand the test of hindsight, ..." (*Review,* V, 1, Summer 1981, pp. 47, 86). Further information is provided by E. Stokes in "The first century of British colonial rule in India: social revolution or social stagnation?" *(Past and Present,* No. 58 (1973), pp. 136-60), and *The Peasant and the Raj* (1978).

Marx's interest in Asia was expressed, for example, in letters to Engels (2 and 14 June, 1853) and in articles he wrote on the British rule in India (10 June and 22 July, 1853). "The basic form of all phenomena in the East ... the absence of private property in land" was, said Marx, "the real key even to the Oriental heaven". He categorically stated that "Indian society has no history at all, at least no known history" and he spoke of "Oriental despotism ... this undignified, stagnatory, and vegetative life," and of "the stationary character of this part of Asia ... stagnant Asiatic despotism." Similarly, in an article on "Chinese Affairs" (7 July 1862) he said that "the Oriental empires always show an unchanging social infrastructure coupled with unceasing change in the persons and tribes who manage to ascribe to themselves the political super-structure." (*Karl Marx on Colonialism and Modernization,* edited and introduced by Shlomo Avineri, 1969, pp. 94, 132, 442, 451, 455-56). In the *Grundrisse* (p. 495) Marx used what Umberto Melotti says is Hegel's expression "the general slavery of the Orient", and in Volume 1 of *Capital* (1977, p. 338) Marx referred to "the unchangeableness of Asiatic societies."

As Avineri indicates (op.cit., pp. 11-12), Marx's basic idea of Oriental societies as unchanging, stagnant, unhistorical (historyless) and despotic follows notions expressed by Hegel, for instance in his *Lectures on the Philosophy of History* (1830-31), about "unhistorical history", despotism, and the lack of historical development in China and India which "remained stationary and fixed". In the same work, black Africa is said to be "no historical part of the world; it has no movement or development to exhibit". (cited by Nathaniel Weyl in *Karl Marx: Racist,* 1979, pp. 75, 81). Iring Fetscher, in an article in *A Dictionary of Marxist Thought* (1985, p. 200), states that Marx "adopts - indeed as a matter of course - Hegel's Eurocentrism."

In his 1859 Preface to *A Contribution to the Critique of Political Economy* Marx introduced the concept of "the Asiatic mode of production" (hereafter AMP) which, says Avineri, has bedevilled Marxism ever since. "In broad outlines", Marx wrote, "Asiatic, ancient, feudal, and modern bourgeois modes of production can be designated as progressive epochs in the economic formation of society." (Marx-Engels, *Selected Works In One Volume,* Moscow/London, 1980, p. 182).

As an article on the subject in the recently published *Dictionary of Marxist Thought* points out, however, Engels did not refer to the AMP in *The Origin of the Family, Private Property and the State* (1884). And moreover, the article continues, there are numerous empirical objections to the application of the AMP to particular societies and the AMP concept is also riddled with theoretical problems. (Paperback edition, 1985, pp. 34-35). Indeed, in *Pre-Capitalist Modes of Production* (1975), Barry Hindess and Paul Hirst say that "no adequate concept of a mode of production corresponding in any way to the notion of the AMP can be developed". (p. 200; see also, by the same authors, *Mode of*

Production and Social Formation, 1977, reprinted 1983, p. 76).

Writing in 1979, the anthropologist Marvin Harris commented: "No general agreement exists as to what Marx meant by infrastructure or the mode of production (Legros, 1979)." Marx "bequeathed a heritage of Hegelian dialectical double talk now being pushed to extremes by new-wave Marxists (to be discussed in Chapter 8)." (*Cultural Materialism: The Struggle for a Science of Culture,* 1980, p. 64). There is a short but lucid and informative chapter on Oriental Despotism and Marx's ideas on the nature of Asian society in Nathaniel Weyl's *Karl Marx: Racist.*

Marx concluded that there was no potential for autonomous social change and development within societies based on the Asiatic mode of production - the required stimulus would come from European conquest and colonialism. This therefore led Marx to endorse European colonial expansion and the destruction of Asiatic society as a brutal but necessary step toward the development of the "barbarous" countries of Asia and its historically progressive consequences. (Umberto Melotti, *Marx and the Third World,* 1977, p. 114; Avineri, op.cit., p. 13; Howard and King, op.cit., 1985, pp. 229-30).

Teleology and the Theory of History

There are some excellent pages in Schwarzschild's book on the Marxian theory of history, comprehensively documented from the writings of Marx and Engels. On page 107 Schwarzschild quotes a passage from *The Holy Family,* written in 1844 by Marx, relating to "the theory of the inevitable decay of the economic system - this theory which was still awaiting proof -" which "was here formulated with the most rigorous precision". This passage, incidentally, is omitted, without any indication being given of this, in the quotation adduced by David McLellan on page 134 of his *Karl Marx: His Life and Thought* (1973 and 1983). "Private property", Marx wrote, "in its economic movement, advances towards its own dissolution, and this through a development which is caused by the very nature of things, and which progresses independent of, unperceived by and against the will of private property". (28) "It was a model, typical Hegelian conception," says Schwarzschild. "Here one could see how the great 'It' [all-powerful driving force], the all-powerful engine, propelled private property with absolutist force towards its predetermined end." A few sentences further on in *The Holy Family* Marx wrote: "It is not a question of what this or that proletarian, or even the whole proletariat, at the moment *regards* as its aim. It is a question of *what the proletarian is,* and what, in accordance with this *being,* it will historically be compelled to do. Its aim and historical action is visibly and irrevocably foreshadowed in its own life situation as well as in the whole organisation of bourgeois society today." (29)

In Volume 1 of *Capital* Marx contended that "Technology ...lays bare the mode of formation of his [man's] social relations, and of the mental conceptions that flow from them". (30) "It is superfluous to add", Marx wrote to Annenkov (28.12.1846), "that men are not free to choose their *productive forces* - which are the basis of all their history - ...". (31) And in *The Poverty of Philosophy* Marx asserts: "The hand-mill gives you society with the feudal lord; the steam-mill, society with the industrial capitalist." (32)

More and more, says Schwarzschild, Marx and Engels came to regard what were pure hypotheses as "laws" - "immanent laws", "universal laws", "absolute laws", "coercive laws", "infallible laws", "compulsory laws", "natural laws which work with iron necessity towards inevitable results". They insisted that they had provided the proof that "history proceeds in the manner of a natural process and is also essentially subject to the same laws of movement". They insisted that they had traced and crystallized the "economic law of motion of modern society", even "the laws of motion of the evolution of humanity". Soon they adopted for this theory the expression "scientific socialism" ... . (op.cit., 1948, pp. 124-25).

The arguments put forward by the communist ideologist and admirer of Stalin, Dr. John Lewis, in *The Marxism of Marx* (1972, pp. 173 and 248), that for Marx there is no inevitability in history, have been shown to be spurious. (33) A. James Gregor, in a masterly series of books and articles (*A Survey of Marxism,* 1965; *The Ideology of Fascism,* 1969; Classical Marxism and the Totalitarian Ethic, 1973, etc.), M.M. Bober (*Karl Marx's Interpretation of History*), Bertram D. Wolfe (*Marxism,* 1967), Karl Kühne (*Economics and Marxism,* Volume 2, 1979, pp. 313-4), the Marxist historian, Eric Hobsbawm, David McLellan (in *Karl Marx : The Legacy,* 1983) (34) have all confirmed or developed points which are raised in Schwarzschild's book.

"Marx himself", says Hobsbawm, "was committed to a specific goal of human history - communism - and a specific role for the proletariat *before* he developed the historical analysis which, as he believed, demonstrated its ineluctability". (35) And Karl Kühne writes: "His [Marx's] research on the 'laws of motion' of capitalism undoubtedly had a teleological purpose: he hoped to establish that the evolution of the economic infrastructure would bring about the overthrow of capitalism and would 'elevate it' into the higher sphere of re-humanised socialism. Here the economist in Marx hands over to the sociologist, the politician and the revolutionary, whose strength derives from his economic vision, which makes him believe in an inevitable victory."

As Gordon Leff says: "whatever its exponents say to the contrary, Marxism is a teleology: the words 'inevitable', 'mission', 'historical destiny', constantly recur in relation to the supersession of capitalism by socialism; they form a continuous theme from the writings of Marx to the present day." (Gordon Leff, *The Tyranny of Concepts: a Critique of Marxism,* Second Edition, 1969, p. 137). In the Introduction to a recent (1986) dictionary of Marxism first published in the United States and Canada, for example, it is asserted that revolution occurs when the productive forces of society come into conflict with its relations of production; that despite the human costs and gains of this process, Marx and Engels argue that such violent and liberatory activities are part of the impersonal evolution of history; and that revolutions are fought because matter makes such conflicts, and the rhetoric which accompanies them, inevitable. (*Biographical Dictionary of Marxism,* Edited by Robert A. Gorman, Mansell Publishing Limited, 1986, pp. 7-8).

Bober and Gregor deal with the much-referred-to letters written by Engels after Marx's death in reaction to the criticism which had descended on the Marxian theory. Engels admitted that Marx and he had laid the main emphasis on the "basic economic facts" and failed to stress enough "the various elements of the superstructure - political forms of the class struggle ... constitutions etc. - forms of law - and then even the reflexes of all these actual struggles in the brains of the combatants: political, legal, philosophical theories, religious ideas ...". The historical event, said Engels, is the resultant of "an infinite series of parallelograms of forces." "Political, juridical, philosophical, religious, literary, artistic, etc. development is based on economic development. But all these react upon one another and also upon the economic base." The geographical basis etc. is included under economic conditions and "race is itself an economic factor." That a so-called great man arises at a particular time in a given country "is of course pure accident. But cut him out and there will be a demand for a substitute" and "the man has always been found as soon as he became necessary ...". It is "rather astonishing", comments Karl Federn, "that Engels did not think of the countless cases in which the great man, the hero who was to save the nation, did not appear." Despite the broadening of the economic interpretation and the admissions made by Engels, he still argued that "the economic movement" is "by far the strongest, most elemental and most decisive" force and "finally asserts itself as necessary"; and that "the economic relations, however much they may be influenced by the other political and ideological ones, are still ultimately the decisive ones, forming the red thread which runs through them and alone leads to understanding." (36)

Bober concludes that "the general impression which these letters make, in common with all the other evidence bearing on the problem, comes to the familiar formula that while institutions and ideas have a part in history, their influence is of such a subordinate character that social events and changes are explicable mainly in terms of economics". (37) But, as Simkhovitch points out in *Marxism Versus Socialism,* "the independent power and influence of our traditions, our political and religious convictions and our various ideologies have been recognized; and no method has been discovered to measure quantitatively the forces of these ideal powers, either absolutely or in relation to the basic economic factor". (38) In Karl Marx's theory of history "we are left", says Professor Duncan, "with evasive, almost vacuous formulations", and some notion of 'basic' or 'determining' causes whose weight and precise effects it becomes difficult to separate out in each particular situation. (39) "Marx and Engels", says Karl Federn, "were the dupes of mere words. ... Marx was unable to free himself from the philosophic training received in his early youth, and his dialectics are no less tainted by scholasticism than those of Hegel." *(The Materialist Conception of History: A Critical Analysis,* 1939, pp. 203, 212).

In a recent (1983) book, Alec Nove comments on the 'reductionist' tendency - identifying one aspect of a problem or situation as its 'essence' - which often accompanies a Marxian view of historical events, and the way in which this attitude leads to mistaken views concerning, for instance, racism and anti-semitism, sexism, alcoholism, crime etc. Quoting from a yet-unpublished work by the émigré Czech sociologist Zdenek Strmiska describing another aspect of 'reductionism', Nove remarks: "This can be seen as one consequence of Marx's philosophical adaptation of Hegel". (40)

As Simkhovitch says (op.cit., pp. 44-45), the view of history worked out by Marx and Engels "was not the offspring of dispassionate research; it was conceived in minds saturated with ideas of social revolution". In a speech in Elberfeld (published August, 1845) Engels argued for communism as an economic necessity and pictured the social revolution as economically unavoidable. "The unavoidable result of our existing social relations," declared Engels, "under all circumstances, and in all cases, will be a *social revolution*. With the same certainty with which we can develop from given mathematical principles a new mathematical proposition, with the same certainty we can deduce from the existing economic relations and the principles of political economy the imminence of social revolution." (Marx-Engels, *Collected Works*, Vol. 4, p.262). Two years or so later Marx and Engels were drafting the *Communist Manifesto*.

Marx's Commodity Fetishism

The dependence of Marx's labour theory of value on a philosophy of "essences" has been traced out by Murray Wolfson in *A Reappraisal of Marxian Economics* (1966). "A commodity", says Marx, is "a very queer thing, abounding in metaphysical subtleties" ... it has a "mystical character". Behind the "outer appearance" of things lies an "invisible and unknown essence", their "inner essence", their "immanent value", "crystals of social substance", amounts of "human labour in the abstract" ... the "equalisation of the most different kinds of labour" ... "embodied or materialised" in commodities. (41)

According to Morishima and Catephores "the concept of abstract labour" is "the basis of the whole labour theory of value". (42) And the notion of abstract labour, says Jerrold Seigel, had appeared in Hegel's *The Philosophy of Right* and Marx had used it too in 1844 in his *Economic and Philosophical Manuscripts*. (43) " 'Marx's economics' ", says Terrell Carver, "is, I think, a misnomer. The essential arguments of these chapters [of *Capital*] are philosophical and logical in character, ..." . (44) "The first chapter of *Capital*", writes Cornelius Castoriadis, "is metaphysical" and Marx's "labour" is "a labour which in truth nobody has ever seen or done." (45)

In a most thorough and closely reasoned analysis of the concept of "human labour in the abstract" in *The Labour Theory of Value in Karl Marx* (46) the logician H.W.B. Joseph shows that in his endeavour to support this conception Marx argues in a circle, and that the whole notion of a homogeneous simple labour to which the most different kinds of specific labour are reducible is erroneous. Homogeneous simple labour is not measurable or indeed observable at all and the amounts of this so-called labour said to be materialised in different articles can only be an assumption. It is essential for Marx's argument, says Joseph, to show that the reduction of the most different kinds of labour to homogeneous simple labour can be made without considering the prices of the commodities; but he cannot show it. If two articles produced by unequal amounts of different specific labour are exchanged or have the same price and this is the only evidence that they embody equal amounts of homogeneous simple labour, Marx simply begs the question and argues in a circle since he professes to find in the quantitative relations between the labours the basis of their respective prices. Marx, adds Joseph, failed to show that in a pre-capitalistic era exchange-relations corresponded to values, and Morishima and Catephores state that "simple commodity production" in which prices gravitate towards Marxian values "has never been realized in history ... even in some tolerably approximate form, because of the lack of sufficient numbers of small independent producers and of sufficient mobility of producers among jobs in the pre-capitalist age." (47)

The notion of "homogeneous human labour" employed by Marx as a basis of value theory is rejected in a recent study by Ulrich Krause, a professor of mathematics (see his *Money and Abstract Labour,* English edn. 1982, pp. 101, 115, 161), as it was by H.W.B. Joseph some 56 years earlier.

Das Kapital: A Project Unfulfilled

As Schwarzschild indicates, when Marx died in 1883 important parts of his analysis of capitalism remained unpublished. There were drafts of material intended for Volumes II, III and IV of *Capital* but in spite of the 16 years that had elapsed since the publication of Volume I in 1867, Marx had still not been able to get his text into order. "Since Volume III was not published in his [Marx's] life-time," says Professor Joan Robinson, "we may suppose that he was not sure that it was satisfactorily worked out. Perhaps the long delay in completing *Capital* was mainly due to the difficulty of absorbing a rising tendency of real-wage rates into the argument." (48) "The world of inner essence, of value and its laws," writes Jerrold Seigel (in *Marx's Fate*), "had no material reality, no actual empirical existence. Whether this world of theory formed a unity with the realm of experience, ... or whether the two spheres instead remained separate and irreconcilable, was the question Marx's economic theory continually posed, but never finally succeeded in answering." (49)

In the main manuscript for Volume III of *Capital,* drafted mostly in 1864-65, Marx endeavoured to bridge the gap between the world of labour values and surplus value and the *real* world of prices and profit. Referring to the Tables used by Marx to illustrate his arguments, Angus Walker comments that "Marx himself does not pretend that [they] are based on empirical evidence or are anything more than an arithmetical exercise composed in the privacy of his own study, ..." (op.cit., p. 133). " 'Underlying values' ", says Nove (op.cit., p. 31), "are invisible magnitudes that neither workers nor capitalists can respond to, for *they* see actual (or expected) *prices* or wages".

In *A Methodological Appraisal of Marxian Economics* (1980) p. 8 ff. Mark Blaug shows how Marx in *Capital* slips in his argument from value-relations to price-relations, treating the labour said to be "embodied or materialised" in commodities, and surplus value, which are not observable entities or behavioural variables, as if they were something concrete and objective. In Professor Nove's view, the explanation of Marx's 'transformation' of values and surplus value into prices and profit used by Ernest Mandel (in his *Marxist Economic Theory*) is "metaphysical". (50) In his Introduction to a recent symposium seeking to defend classical Marxism (*Ricardo, Marx, Sraffa,* 1984) (51) Mandel remarks on "some differences between the authors which have not been ironed out, despite several fruitful conferences ...". Mandel refers to the "transformation problem" in the third volume of Marx's *Capital* and says that "Anwar

Shaikh's contribution to the present volume, ... nevertheless concludes that the sum of profit can and generally does differ from the sum of surplus-value." In the third volume of *Capital,* however, Marx states that "the sum of the profits in all spheres of production must equal the sum of the surplus-values." (*Capital,* Vol. III (1977), Part II Chap.X. p. 173). This denial of one of Marx's formulas evidently contradicts the argument used by Mandel which Mandel feels "flows from the basic assumptions of Marxist economic theory: ... ". A critical appraisal of some of these assumptions and of Marx's *Capital* may be found in Chapters 12 and 15 of Schwarzschild's book. Subsequently published works providing further detailed, critical analysis of Marxian economics include Mark Blaug's brilliant *Economic Theory in Retrospect* (4th edition, 1985) and Karl Pribram's monumental work of scholarship, *A History of Economic Reasoning* (1983). (52)

The "Accumulation of Misery"

In Chapter 15 (pp. 300 ff.) of his book Schwarzschild considers "Marx's old contention" that the capitalist system brings about progressively "increasing misery" and what Marx claims in Volume 1 of *Capital* to have revealed as the hidden causes and inherent characteristics in capitalism which produce this phenomenon. Schwarzschild gives a list of examples of "all the different forms which the growing misery will take" according to Marx such as "lengthening of the working-day", "progressive production of a relative surplus-population or industrial reserve army" [i.e. the unemployed, paupers etc.], "squeezing out more labour in a given time ... by increasing the speed of the machinery, and by giving the workman more machinery to tend", "systematic robbery of what is necessary for the life of the workman while he is at work, robbery of space, light, air, and of protection to his person", "the adulteration of food", "the deterioration of human labour-power ... the premature exhaustion and death of this labour-power itself." (*Capital,* Vol. 1, 1977, pp. 384-85, 589-92, 388, 402, 563, 253).

Schwarzschild includes "A continual drop in wages" among the various facets of the "increasing misery" although he adds that "It can happen that here and there wages will rise. But as soon as 'accumulation slackens in consequence of the rise in the price of labour, ... The price of labour falls again' ". (*Capital,* Vol. 1, 1977, pp. 580-81).

Schwarzschild gives a number of other quotations from Volume 1 of *Capital* to support this. "The constant tendency of capital is to force the cost of labour back towards this zero." "The more extensive, finally, the lazarus-layers of the working-class, and the industrial reserve army, the greater is official pauperism. *This is the absolute general law of capitalist accumulation.*" "It was constantly pre-supposed that wages are at least equal to the value of labour-power. Forcible reduction of wages below this value plays, however, in practice too important a part, for us not to pause upon it for a moment." (ibid., pp. 562, 603). On page 300 of his book Schwarzschild says that "The entire object of" *Capital* "is to prove scientifically why capitalism has been, and always will be, condemned to make people progressively poorer." And on page 301 he quotes Marx as stating in Volume 1 of *Capital* that "In proportion as capital accumulates, the lot of the labourer must grow worse". But what Marx actually wrote was that "the lot of the labourer, be his payment high or low, must grow worse". This wording is given, for instance, in editions of Volume 1 of *Capital* published in 1891 (cited by Simkhovitch, op. cit., p. 119), 1932 (*Capital And Other Writings,* The Modern Library, p. 182) and 1977 (p. 604).

It seems, however, to be "wrong", says Ronald L. Meek, "to place too much emphasis on the words 'be his payment high or low' " in this passage in Volume 1 of *Capital.* (*Economics And Ideology And Other Essays* (Part Two, "Marx's 'Doctrine Of Increasing Misery' "), 1967, p. 122). In his enunciation of what has been called the "doctrine of increasing misery" in Chapters XXV and XXXII of Volume 1, Marx writes of "agony of toil, slavery, ignorance, brutality, mental degradation" and of "oppression, slavery, degradation, exploitation". There is little direct reference in these passages, says Meek, to the question of the general wage level; or, as Louis B. Boudin puts it (*The Theoretical System of Karl Marx,* 1910, p. 220), "Marx does not speak of the growth of the poverty of the working class." But, as Meek goes on to point out, when Marx proceeds - in Section 5 of Chapter XXV - to give what he calls "Illustrations Of The General Law Of Capitalist Accumulation" (*Capital,* Volume 1, 1977, p. 607), the question of the behaviour of wages is by no means left out of account. "For a full elucidation of the law of accumulation", says Marx, "his [the labourer's] condition outside the workshop must also be looked at, his condition as to food and dwelling. The limits of this book compel us to concern ourselves chiefly with the worst paid part of the industrial proletariat, and with the agricultural labourers, who together form the majority of the working-class." Thus, Marx's views "about the behaviour of wages should properly be regarded as constituent parts of, or at any rate as assumptions underlying, his 'doctrine of increasing misery' ". (Meek, op.cit., 1967, p. 117).

Meek (1967) and M.C. Howard & J.E. King (in the first edition of *The political economy of Marx,* 1975) are equally critical of an article by Thomas Sowell on "Marx's 'Increasing Misery' Doctrine" (*The American Economic Review,* March 1960). Referring to "Marx's picture of the worker at subsistence", Sowell states that "Once a new higher standard of living becomes established, it too becomes subsistence, and represents the new value of labour-power, i.e. the real-wage level. ... Far from being a law of increasing misery in the conventional sense, it represents a law of a customary floor under wages, which would *prevent* such an occurrence." Commenting on this, Meek says that "If the value of labour-power at any given time is taken to be simply what the workers happen to have been getting for their labour-power during the previous few years, Marx's theory of wages becomes so general as to be virtually meaningless." (op.cit., 1967, p.119). And Howard and King declare that "Sowell's argument is weak, both conceptually and empirically". They also refer to a danger, from Marx's point of view, in a bargaining power theory of wages, of defining "subsistence" in terms of wages, thus explaining the value of labour power in terms of wages, rather than vice versa. And their conclusions are that "Unless we are prepared to resort to a tautological *identification* of the real wage and the value of labour power, Marx's attempt to integrate the labour theory of value with the theory of wages must be judged a failure, and the theory of income distribution remains an open question. ... We must agree with Meek (1967, p. 124) that there is no way in which Marx's predictions can be reconciled with the actual course of real wages over the last century." (op.cit., 1975, p. 135).

Sowell has now published a book entitled *Marxism: Philosophy and Economics* (1985) which, he says, compared to his earlier writings on Marx, "draws on additional knowledge, later scholarship by others, newly unearthed facts and more recently translated work ... ." The book includes two sections on the " 'Increasing misery' of the proletariat" (pp. 125-133 and 201-203) and in an assessment at the end of the book Sowell says that in professional economics "*Capital* was a detour into a blind alley, however historic it may be as the centrepiece of a worldwide political movement;" and he refers to "people who have never read through it, much less followed its labyrinthine reasoning from its arbitrary postulates to its empirically false conclusions." (p. 217).

As stated by Meek (1967), the "general law of capitalist accumulation" as Marx envisaged it, "manifested itself not only in the formation of a growing number of poverty-stricken unemployed, not only in increasing exploitation, increasing fragmentation of the human personality, etc., but also in a very low material standard of living, i.e., roughly, in very low real wages for the great majority of the employed workers." (pp. 121-122). Meek quotes Engels's Introduction of 1891 to Marx's *Wage Labour and Capital:* "From the whole mass of products produced by it, the working class, therefore, only receives a part for itself. ... the part falling to the working class (reckoned per head) either increases only very slowly and inconsiderably or not at all, and under certain circumstances may even fall." (Marx-Engels, *Selected Works In One Volume,* 1980, p. 70). But, as Bober says (op.cit., 1965, p. 219), "Marx does not fail to produce declarations that run with the hares and hunt with the hounds." Whilst, Meek claims, "there is absolutely no evidence," at any rate in Marx's mature economic writings, "of a belief that real wages per head would show a long-run tendency to decline," Marx "expected 'relative' wages (i.e. labour's share in the national income) to fall." (op.cit., 1967, p. 117). In *Capital* (Vol. 1, Part V, Chap. XVII, I, 1977, p. 490) Marx says that "it is possible with an increasing productiveness of labour, for the price of labour-power to keep on falling, and yet this fall to be accompanied by a constant growth in the mass of the labourer's means of subsistence. But even in such case, ... the abyss between the labourer's position and that of the capitalist would keep widening."

Marx, says Meek, "believed that there were certain important 'non-economic' respects in which the lot of the labourer would grow worse even if his real wages rose," and that "any rise in real wages which in fact took place would be too slow and inconsiderable to provide an appreciable offset to the misery-increasing effects of these 'non-economic' factors" and of the fall in "relative" wages which Marx expected as capitalism developed. Thus, Meek thinks we may "quite fairly impute to Marx something like a doctrine of 'increasing relative misery' in the purely economic sphere ... there is little doubt that Marx did anticipate that as capitalism developed *relative* wages would decline, whatever happened to *absolute* wages." In fact, however, says Meek, "the rise in real wages which has actually taken place in the advanced capitalist countries since Marx's time is much greater than that which Marx anticipated" and "the appreciable fall in 'relative wages' which Marx anticipated has not ... taken place." (op.cit., 1967, pp. 117, 120-123).

Ernest Mandel (*Marxist Economic Theory*, 1977, p. 17) and Anwar Shaikh (*A Dictionary of Marxist Thought*, 1985, p. 362) refer to "relative impoverishment" although, according to Mark Blaug (*Economic Theory in Retrospect*, 4th Edition, 1985, p. 257), Marx "never used the phrase". And Mandel flatly contradicts himself in referring to the theory of "absolute impoverishment" which, he says, has been falsely attributed to Marx. In *Marxist Economic Theory* (1968, 4th impression 1977, pp. 150-51) Mandel asserts that: "The 'theory of absolute impoverishment' is not to be found in the works of Marx. ... The idea that the real wages of the workers tend to decline more and more is totally alien to Marx's writings; ... ." But in his Introduction to the Penguin Books edition of Volume 1 of *Capital* (1976. Reprinted 1982) Mandel states that: "Marx, in his youthful writings, did in fact hold such a theory - for example, in the Communist Manifesto." On pages 69-70 of this Introduction Mandel writes: "How, then, has it been possible for so many writers, for so long, to have attributed to Marx a 'theory of absolute impoverishment of the workers under capitalism' which obviously implied a theory of tendential fall in the value not only of labour-power but even of real wages? In the first place because Marx, in his youthful writings, did in fact hold such a theory - for example, in the Communist Manifesto."

Mandel refers to two passages in the *Manifesto*, one of which (given on p. 78 of Karl Marx, *The Revolutions of 1848*, Penguin Books, 1981) is commented on, in a footnote, by Meek who is of the opinion that it "clearly refers to the growth of the reserve army of labour and thus of 'pauperism' ". And Meek adds that to find any statement in Marx's writing which could reasonably be interpreted as implying a prediction of declining real wages we would have "to go right back to Marx's *Economic and Philosophic Manuscripts of 1844* (see, e.g., *Manuscripts*, (Moscow, 1959), pp. 66 and 69)."

Bob Rowthorn, however in his *Capitalism, Conflict And Inflation*

(Lawrence and Wishart, 1980) discusses Marx's early writings in the period 1847-8 on the question of wages, including Marx's manuscript on *Wages* (1847) which was first published in English in 1976, and the passage in the *Communist Manifesto* referred to by Mandel and Meek. And Rowthorn's conclusion is that: "In view of these and other passages, there is no doubt that, at this time, Marx and indeed Engels believed in the thesis of absolute impoverishment, that wages would be forced down to their physiological minimum. This proposition was later popularized by Ferdinand Lassalle as the notorious 'iron law of wages', and became the subject of bitter dispute within the German Socialist movement. By then, however, both Marx and Engels had changed their opinion and were harshly critical of Lassalle." (op.cit., p. 194).

In the *Ecomomic and Philosophic Manuscripts* (1959, p. 69) Marx declared: "We proceed from an *actual* economic fact. The worker becomes all the poorer the more wealth he produces, the more his production increases in power and range."

In the manuscript on *Wages* (December, 1847) which, as stated in a Note in the Marx-Engels *Collected Works* completes Marx's *Wage-Labour and Capital* but which Marx had no time to prepare for the press, Marx wrote: " ... the minimum wage is determined on average by the price of the most indispensable provisions, ... The minimum itself has a historical movement and sinks always further towards the absolutely lowest level. ... When wages have once fallen and later rise again, they never rise, however, to their previous level. In the course of development, there is a double fall in wages: *Firstly:* relative, in proportion to the development of general wealth. *Secondly:* absolute, since the quantity of commodities which the worker receives in exchange becomes less and less." (Marx-Engels, *Collected Works,* Volume 6, 1976, pp. 425-26, 693; see also Volume 9, 1977, p. 560).

And in a *Speech On The Question Of Free Trade* (delivered January 9, 1848 and published in French in February 1848) Marx said: "what is the minimum of wages? Just so much as is required for production of the articles absolutely necessary for the maintenance of the worker, for the continuation, by hook or by crook, of his own existence and that of his class. ... That is to say that within a given time which recurs periodically, ... when reckoning all that the working class has had above and below mere necessaries, we shall see that, after all, they have received neither more nor less than the minimum; ... But this is not all. The progress of industry creates less and less expensive means of subsistence. ... Thus, as means are constantly being found for the maintenance of labor on cheaper and more wretched food, the minimum of wages is constantly sinking." (*Collected Works,* Volume 6, pp. 462-63).

It does not, however, seem to be correct to say, as does Bertram D. Wolfe in his *Marxism* (1967, p. 323), that in Volume One of *Das Kapital* "Marx has not one word to say on the movement of wages in England after 1850!" The English edition (1887) of Volume One of *Das Kapital* was translated from the third German edition of 1883 which was prepared with the assistance of notes left by the author. And in Part VII, Chapter XXV, Section 3, for example, it is stated that: "Between 1849 and 1859, a rise of wages practically insignificant, though accompanied by falling prices of corn, took place in the English agricultural districts." (Swan Sonnenschein & Co., Ltd., London, Twelfth impression, February, 1908, p. 652).

As Rowthorn says, "the theory of wages has for long been a subject of intense debate between Marxists and others, and amongst Marxists themselves." Most Marxists "have only the haziest idea of what Marx actually said about wages, ... Even works of considerable scholarship, dealing with the character and evolution of Marx's views, are inadequate and sometimes very inaccurate in their treatment of wages. For example, Roman Rosdolsky's famous book *The Making Of Marx's Capital* ...". And "like Rosdolsky", Ernest Mandel "does not really confront the main theoretical issues involved." In his "CONCLUSION" Rowthorn says that: "Marx's writings on wages are extremely uneven and do not form a coherent and consistent whole. ... even if we confine ourselves to the later so-called 'mature' works, such as *Capital* or *Wages, Price and Profit,* we find the same incoherence and inconsistency." (op.cit., pp. 182,225).

In *Economics And Ideology And Other Essays,* Professor Meek points out that Marx's prediction of the "increasing misery" of the working class was no minor or incidental part of Marx's analysis but an essential constituent of his general theory of the transition from capitalism to communism. It was above all what Marx described in Volume 1 of *Capital* (Chap. XXV. Section 4, 1983, p. 603) as "the misery of constantly extending strata of the active army of labour, and the dead weight of pauperism" which would impel the working class to decisive revolutionary action.

But, says Meek, the prediction of "increasing misery" is "not the only one of Marx's predictions which has been falsified by the facts." Citing Joseph Gillman's summarization (in *The Falling Rate of Profit*, New York, 1958, p. 1) of Marx's most famous and most crucial "laws of motion of capitalism", Meek says that in Marx's opinion it was largely through the operation of these "laws of motion", and particularly the law of the increasing misery of the working class, that capitalism would reach its historical limits. Yet, Meek writes, "of these four laws I think it is fair to say that during the last half-century only the third [i.e. the law of concentration and centralization of capital] has manifested itself on the surface of reality in a reasonably unambiguous manner, at any rate in the more advanced capitalist countries. In the case of the other three laws [i.e. the law of the tendency of the rate of profit to fall; the law of the increasing severity of cyclical crises; the law of the increasing misery of the working class], things have by and large turned out to be substantially different from what Marx expected." (Meek, op.cit., pp. 126-27).

In *Marxist Sociology Revisited* (1985), David Booth draws attention to "a basic problem with Marxist theory as an input to development sociology which transcends the particular forms in which it has been manifested. This is its metatheoretical commitment to demonstrating that what happens in societies in the era of capitalism is not only explicable but also in some stronger sense *necessary* . ... Reality has shown itself too rich to be captured by the simple terms of a concept of relations of production with corresponding 'laws of motion', and relations of production with wholly non-corresponding laws of motion are a theoretical nonsense." (*Marxist Sociology Revisited: Critical Assessments*, Edited by Martin Shaw, 1985, Chapter 3, pp. 74,77).

How Marx Used the British Parliamentary Blue Books

In his book *Labouring Men* (1964, reissued in paperback 1986, pp. 245-46) the Marxist historian, Professor E.J. Hobsbawm, remarks on a paper by J.R. Tanner and F.S. Carey published by the Cambridge Economic Club, May Term, 1885. The title of this paper is "Comments on the Use of the Blue Books made by Karl Marx in Chapter XV of 'Le Capital' " i.e. the French edition of Marx's major work.

A French edition of Volume One of Marx's *Capital* was produced in separate parts between 1872 and 1875 and as stated on the title-page it was "Completely revised by the author." This French edition, Marx claimed, "possesses a scientific value independent of the original and should be consulted even by readers familiar with German." (*Karl Marx: A Biography*, Moscow, Second revised edition, 1977, pp. 402-3).

What Professor Hobsbawm finds "interesting" in Tanner and Carey's paper, from which he quotes a few phrases, is "the tone of denigration rather than the content of this work." He does not say that Tanner and Carey make a series of detailed comparisons between the original Blue Books and statements for which Marx claims the authority of these Government Reports. Neither does Professor Hobsbawm give, or refer to, a single, specific example from the list of comparisons made by Tanner and Carey between Marx and the Blue Books. Yet he suggests that the two authors were "unfair" in their attitude to Marx.

As stated by Tanner and Carey, however, near the beginning of their paper: "The writers of these pages first examined Marx's references to derive fuller information on some points discussed in 'Le Capital' than that contained in the text, and then being struck as they went on with accumulating discrepancies, they determined to settle if possible the scope and importance of the errors so plainly existing. It was soon clear to them that the differences were not the result of inaccuracy solely, that they were too vital to be included in any list of errata and addenda; indeed throughout the inaccuracies showed signs of a distorting influence."

Some of the examples of Marx's method of work given by Tanner and Carey, together with textual evidence, are as follows:-

Pages 7-8: "There is another class of cases in which reference to the Reports shows that quotations from them have often been conveniently shortened by the omission of passages which would be likely to weigh against the conclusion which Marx was trying to establish. We print below an extract from *Marx*, ... with the suppressed passage restored:- ... In this case, not only is the italicised passage omitted, but the quotation is allowed to run on continuously, and the existence of the omitted passage is not indicated in any way."

Pages 8-9: " 'Le Capital' chapter XV also contains instances of another kind of misrepresentation more serious than any that have been yet quoted. It consists in piecing together fictitious quotations out of isolated statements contained in different parts of a Report. These are then foisted upon the reader in inverted commas with all the authority of direct quotations from the Blue Books themselves. For instance:- ... By this method of constructing evidence he [Marx] is led into what almost amounts to falsification. Thus:- .... Another instance occurs on the same page:- .... The remainder of the paragraph, though put within inverted commas, is fabricated from a number of isolated statements selected at random from nn. 217 and 220."

Page 10: "In Marx's treatment of the influence of the sewing machine, however, he uses the Blue Books with a recklessness which is appalling, and uses them to prove just the contrary of what they really establish. This will be most conveniently exhibited by printing in parallel columns a passage from Marx, and an abstract of three of the references to the Reports on which it is ostensibly founded. ..."

Based on the results of this detailed examination of various particular cases, the general conclusion arrived at by Tanner and Carey is that: "The detailed comparisons we have made may not be sufficient to sustain a charge of deliberate falsification against the author of 'Le Capital', especially since falsification seems so unnecessary; but they certainly seem to us to show an almost criminal recklessness in the use of authorities which warrants us in regarding other parts of Marx's work with suspicion ."

Evidence of the way in which Marx falsified the sense of Gladstone's budget speech of 1863, by piecing together selected parts of sentences which appear in reports of the speech and omitting words preceding and intervening, is given later in the present work. This account is based on publications by David Felix (1983) and Chushichi Tsuzuki (1967). Attention is also drawn to some respects in which "Marx uses and distorts [Adam] Smith's views for his own polemical purposes." (Michael Evans, op.cit. (Note 5), May 1984, p. 144). According to Professor Raddatz, Marx's system of making extracts is highly indicative of his mental makeup. He did not in some instances copy out or translate correctly passages which he extracted - by a sort of polemical method of collation he created an atmosphere of antipathy; by this method he infused into these extracts precisely what he needed later for an aggressive system of argumentation - based on these "sources". (Fritz J. Raddatz, *Karl Marx: A Political Biography*, 1979, p. 147.)

Marx and the Trade Unions

Schwarzschild makes a few references to Marx's opinions on trade unions and English trade union leaders (see, e.g. pp. 311, 346). A. Lozovsky's *Marx and the Trade Unions* (1935) is written by a Soviet author but some useful material may be gleaned from it. In June 1865, at two meetings of the General Council of the International Working Men's Association, Marx read a paper on the question of wage increases and trade unions etc. His arguments incorporated part of his materials for *Capital* (cf. Schwarzschild, pp. 300 ff). Marx's manuscript was written in English and this work can therefore be read without the mediation of translator or interpreter. It was found among Marx's papers after Engels's death and was first published in 1898, under the auspices of Marx's daughter Eleanor and Edward Aveling, as an individual work entitled *Value, Price and Profit.* It has since been published under the title *Wages, Price and Profit.*

Marx concluded that: "The general tendency of capitalist production is not to raise, but to sink the average standard of wages." Trades Unions "work well as centres of resistance against the encroachments of capital" but the working class ought not to forget that "they are retarding the downward movement, but not changing its direction." They ought to inscribe on their banner "the *revolutionary* watchword, '*Abolition of the wages system!'* " (Marx-Engels, *Selected Works*, Vol. 2 (1977), pp. 74-75).

In the *1844 Manuscripts* (1959, p. 66) Marx wrote that "Eventually wages, which have already been reduced to a minimum, must be reduced yet further, to meet the new competition. This then necessarily leads to revolution." According to Engels: "In war the injury of one party is the benefit of the others, and since workingmen are on a war footing towards their employers, they do merely what great potentates do when they seize each other by the throat. ... These strikes, ... are the school of war of the workingmen in which they prepare themselves for the great struggle which cannot be avoided; ...". (*The Condition of the Working-Class in England,* quoted by Lozovsky (1935) pp.121-122; cf. Marx-Engels, *Collected Works,* Vol. 4, pp. 510,512). And Engels continued: "As schools of war, the Unions are unexcelled. ... The war of the poor against the rich will be the bloodiest ever waged. ... The revolution must come; it is already too late to bring about a peaceful solution; ... ." (*Collected Works,* Vol. 4, pp. 512,581).

The "Plan of War Against Democracy"

On page 224 of *The Red Prussian* (1948) Schwarzschild gives a quotation from the March 1850 *Address of the Central Authority to the [Communist] League.* This document, written by Marx and Engels, was, as Marx said in a letter to Engels (13 July, 1851), "at bottom nothing but a plan of war against democracy". (53) Schwarzschild refers to this on p. 177. "Although little known and rarely studied," says Robert Payne (*Marx,* p.239), the March 1850 *Address* is "one of the most important and seminal documents of the 19th century."

A note on page 674 of Volume 10 (1978) of the Marx-Engels *Collected Works* states that the *Address* "contained fundamental propositions of the Marxist programme and tactics". There is a most interesting account, by Bertram D. Wolfe, of the *Address* and the *Communist Manifesto* in *Marxism: 100 Years in the Life of a Doctrine* (1967) and in *Marxism in the Modern World* (edited by Milorad M. Drachkovitch, 1965). The *Address* (or *Circular Letter*), says Wolfe (*Marxism,* p. 19), "is noteworthy both for the extremism of the methods advocated to secure its aims and the highly statist and centralist formulation of those aims".

The programme and tactics recommended by Marx and Engels included: "secret and public organisation of the workers' party" - "arming of the whole proletariat" - taking the lead in "so-called excesses, instances of popular revenge against hated individuals or public buildings" - setting up "revolutionary municipal councils" - establishing "revolutionary workers' governments ... alongside the new official governments". The workers must: "compel the democrats ... to compromise themselves" and "to concentrate the utmost possible productive forces, means of transport, factories, railways, etc., in the hands of the state" - strive "for the most determined centralisation of power in the hands of the state authority" - "carry to the extreme the proposals of the democrats" and outbid them in every demand for social reform by putting forward a more extreme demand - "dictate such conditions" to the democrats that their rule "will from the outset bear within it the seeds of its downfall". (54) The *March Address*, says Payne, "acted like a bomb with a delayed fuse, exploding only in the twentieth century."

Marx and the Theory of the State

In the *Communist Manifesto* Marx and Engels declared that "The executive of the modern State is but a committee for managing the common affairs of the whole bourgeoisie. ... Political power, properly so called, is merely the organised power of one class for oppressing another." (*Collected Works*, Vol. 6, pp. 486,505).

In his 1859 Preface to *A Contribution to the Critique of Political Economy* Marx wrote: "My inquiry led to the conclusion that neither legal relations nor forms of state could be grasped whether by themselves or on the basis of a so-called general development of the human mind, but on the contrary they have their origin in the material conditions of existence, the totality of which Hegel ... embraces within the term 'civil society'; that the anatomy of this civil society, however, has to be sought in political economy." (Peking, 1976, pp. 2-3).

Again, in 1887, in the second edition of *The Housing Question*, which first appeared in the form of articles in 1872-3, Engels reiterated that "The state is nothing but the organised collective power of the possessing classes, the landowners and the capitalists, as against the exploited classes, the peasants and the workers." (Marx-Engels, *Selected Works*, Vol. 2 (1977), p. 347).

Professor Leonard Krieger has, however, drawn attention - in an article on "Marx And Engels As Historians" - to "the difficulty which Marx and Engels experienced in digesting the contemporary history of the Revolution of 1848." (*Journal of the History of Ideas*, Vol. XIV, No. 3, June 1953, p. 402). Just before Marx began writing *The Eighteenth Brumaire of Louis Bonaparte* he sent Engels a letter (9 December 1851) in which he openly admitted: "I have kept you waiting for an answer, quite bewildered [in English] by the tragicomic sequence of events in France." (*Collected Works*, Vol. 38 (1982), p.507). Engels had written to Marx on 3 December 1851, a day after Louis Bonaparte, President of the French Republic, carried out his *coup d'état*, and Hal Draper comments that Engels's letter was punctuated by words like *comedy, farce, silly, infantile, stupid* and "there was no hint of an insight into what had taken place." (*Karl Marx's Theory Of Revolution*, Vol. 1, p. 403).

Krieger refers to "the frustration of the hopes he [Marx] had drawn from his interpretation of contemporary French history in the first three sections of *The Class Struggles in France*. ... the repeated expressions of bewilderment over the post revolutionary French developments in the correspondence between Marx and Engels, Marx's return to economic studies during 1850 in the attempt to find explanations not vouchsafed by his historical labors, and finally the tremendous effort made [by Marx] in the *Contribution to the Critique of Political Economy* and *Capital* to translate the specific forms of 'consciousness' which go to make up history into a malleable mass automatically explicable by his theory." (op. cit., pp. 383, 402-3).

Engels summed up the theory of the state shortly after Marx's death: "... it is, as a rule, the state of the most powerful, economically dominant class, ... the modern representative state is an instrument of exploitation of wage-labour by capital. ... the state, which in all typical periods is exclusively the state of the ruling class ... ." But Engels gave several examples in which "By way of exception, however, periods occur in which the warring classes balance each other so nearly that the state power, as ostensible mediator, acquires for the moment a certain degree of independence of both." (*The Origin of the Family, Private Property and the State*, 1884, Fourth German edition 1891. Marx-Engels *Selected Works*, Vol. 3, 1977, pp. 328-29, 332).

The exceptional periods adduced by Engels included the régimes of Napoleon I, Louis Bonaparte and Bismarck. According to Draper these were "all autonomized states resting on an equilibrium of contending class forces", tending "to assert autonomy from the ruling classes to a greater or lesser extent." And Draper adds that the first example given by Engels - the absolute monarchy of the 17th and 18th centuries - involved an autonomized state i.e. a state which "cuts loose from its foundations in civil society", not, as Engels said, "for the moment" but for a whole historical era in a number of different countries. (op.cit., pp. 461, 464-65). Or, as Kenneth Minogue puts it (in *Alien Powers*, 1985, p. 206), Engels's mind, so suitable to dialectical reasoning, provides us with one doctrine by assertion and its contradictory by exemplification.

According to Professor Jon Elster, "In Marx's political writings from the 1850's we repeatedly encounter the idea that the state serves the interest of the capitalist class, without being the direct extension of its will as the earlier writings had argued." State autonomy "may be explained by the fact that it is useful for the economically dominant class" because "they perceive that their interests are better served if they remain outside politics" - or "it may be allowed by the fact that there is no single dominant class" permitting "the government to play an active rule [? role] by mediation and divide-and-conquer." Elster's view is that a "class-balance theory of the state" has "some claim to be considered as Marx's *general* theory of the modern state. ... To conclude, it is hardly too much to say that Marx made the autonomy of the state into the cornerstone of his theory." Thus, as against what Engels said was "in all typical periods" the "rule," Professor Elster now says that "it is difficult to escape the conclusion that what in Marxist theory is supposed to be the 'normal case' - the subservience of the state to the interests of the bourgeoisie - is only exceptionally realized" and "An essence that makes such rare appearances on the historical scene cannot be that essential." (*Making Sense of Marx*, 1985, pp. 405-06, 411, 422, 426-28).

In *The Social Sciences Since the Second World War* (1982, p.9), Daniel Bell refers to the question of the "autonomy of politics", and the independent role of a State over and above individual capitalist groups, or even of capitalists to save capitalism, as a theme that has preoccupied neo-Marxist writers, such as Ralph Miliband and Nicos Poulantzas. What is striking in their work, says Bell, is the lack of any empirical or historical study, so that the "debates" become essentially textual and scholastic.

In a chapter on "Neutrality and the State" in *Alien Powers*, Minogue critically discusses the view of the state presented by Marx and Engels and their intellectual descendants and examines passages from the work of such writers as David McLellan, Ralph Miliband, and Nicos Poulantzas. Minogue makes explicit a feature of ideological argument - the technique of making dramatic statements of the 'being determines thought' type and subsequently modifying such doctrines almost out of recognition by a steady incorporation of qualifications to deal with realities to which the doctrines are not adequate. This back-pedalling exemplified in classical Marxism, says Professor Minogue, has become a byword in serious social thought for intellectual muddle, but variations of it can be found in much academic argument.

The "intellectual muddle", "discordant notes", and "incredibly naive and Utopian" notions in the writings of Marx and Engels on the state have been remarked on by Bober, Nove, Minogue and others. In *The State In Captialist Europe: A Casebook* (edited by Stephen Bornstein, David Held and Joel Krieger, 1984), Held and Krieger's judgment is that Marx never developed an adequate theory of the relationship among class, bureaucracy and state. He "left a thoroughly ambiguous heritage, never fully reconciling his understanding of the state as an instrument of class domination with his acknowledgement that the state might also have significant political independence." (p.1).

Marx's Notes on Bakunin

Marx claimed to have proved that "the class struggle necessarily leads to the *dictatorship of the proletariat*" which "itself only constitutes the transition to the *abolition of all classes* and to a *classless society.*" But, as stated by the historian A.J.P. Taylor in his Introduction to the Pelican edition of the *Communist Manifesto* (1985, p. 34), Marx had not proved the second point at all and could prove the first point "only by relying on the dialectic."

Schwarzschild was familiar with E.H. Carr's book *Michael Bakunin* (1937) but Carr does not mention Bakunin's *Statism and Anarchy,* written in Russian and published in 1873, which expressed aversion to Marx's theory of proletarian rule which Bakunin contended would in fact mean "the despotism of the *ruling minority*": "Hence the result is that the vast majority of the people is governed by a privileged minority. ... it may perhaps consist of former workmen, but as soon as they become representatives or rulers of the people they *cease to be workmen* and view all ordinary workers from the eminence of state; they will then no longer represent the people, but only themselves and their pretensions to govern the people."

Marx (in 1874-75) copied out passages from Bakunin's book and then added his own rejoinders on each passage so that it reads like a dialogue. Whilst not published in Marx's lifetime these extracts and comments were published in Russia in 1926 as "Comments on Bakunin's Book, *Statehood and Anarchy.*"

In the *Communist Manifesto* and elsewhere there are references to "the proletariat organised as the ruling class" and Bakunin raised a very important issue by asking: "What is meant by the proletariat transformed into the ruling class? Will perhaps the proletariat as a whole head the government?" The Germans, said Bakunin, "number nearly 40 million. Will, for example, all 40 million be members of the government?" Marx's response to this question fails to carry conviction. He replied: "Certainly, for the thing begins with the self-government of the commune." On other extracts from Bakunin's book, Marx commented: "... when class rule has disappeared a state in the now accepted political sense of the word no longer exists. ... (1) government functions no longer exist; (2) the distribution of general functions becomes a routine matter and does not entail any domination; (3) elections completely lose their present political character." (Marx-Engels-Lenin, *Anarchism and Anarcho-Syndicalism*, 1974, pp. 150-52).

In a review in *Telos* (No. 59, Spring 1984) of a book by Paul Thomas on *Karl Marx and the Anarchists,* Graham Baugh refers to "Bakunin's dire and prescient predictions of Marxist authoritarianism which Noam Chomsky has described as 'perhaps among the most remarkable within the social sciences' ". These predictions, says Baugh, are dismissed by Thomas as "wilful exaggerations, or even fantasies. ... In *Karl Marx and the Anarchists* propaganda masquerades as scholarship. Often, arguments are replaced by epithets and factual distortions. ... His [Thomas's] treatment of Marx rarely goes beyond devotion. On the whole, *Karl Marx and the Anarchists* is not a credible book."

A century after Marx wrote his comments on *Statism and Anarchy,* the failure of his "massively Utopian construction" to carry conviction has been noted by a number of commentators including Michael Evans (*Karl Marx,* 1975, pp. 156-57), Radoslav Selucký (*Marxism, Socialism, Freedom,* 1979, pp. 79-80). Peter Singer (*Marx,* 1980, pp. 75-6), and Jon Elster (*Making Sense of Marx*, 1985, pp. 456-58). See also Alec Nove (op.cit., 1983, pp. 46-50, 55-60).

Michael Evans, for instance, notes the way in which the word "proletariat", as in the term "the dictatorship of the proletariat," expands and contracts according to context in Marx's writings, and that "the rise of new middle groupings also helps to complicate the picture." He points out that whereas Marx replies to Bakunin's question about proletarian rule by saying that "the whole thing begins with the self-government of the commune," in "a France where the majority still worked in agriculture and many were still small proprietors, ... no socialist policy could have been implemented, for the communes would have been peasant-dominated." And in Volume III of *Capital* (1977, Part VI, Chap. XLVII, Section V, p. 813) Marx himself states that "small landed property creates a class of barbarians standing halfway outside of society." Schwarzschild, who makes very similar observations to those later made by Evans, comments on the "remarkable contradictions" in which Marx and Engels involved themselves. (op.cit., pp. 151-52, 185). In *The Civil War in France* (1871), in an account of the political structure within the Paris Commune, Marx says that the peasants were brought under the lead of the urban workers who were "the natural trustees of their interests." Quoting this, Evans remarks (op.cit., pp. 152, 197-footnote 228) that "Marx is disingenuous here. As we have seen, he was aware of the antagonism between proletarian and peasant."

In his essay "Indifference to Politics", written and published in 1873, Marx refers to the political struggle assuming "violent forms" and to the workers substituting "their revolutionary dictatorship for the dictatorship of the bourgeois class" in order to "crush the resistance of the bourgeoisie," thus giving the State "a revolutionary and transient form." And in a companion essay "On Authority", Engels writes: "A revolution is certainly the most authoritarian thing there is; ... the victorious party ... must maintain this rule by means of the terror which its arms inspire in the reactionaries. Would the Paris Commune have lasted a single day if it had not made use of this authority of the armed people against the bourgeois? Should we not, on the contrary, reproach it for not having used it freely enough?" (in *Anarchism and Anarcho-Syndicalism*, 1974, pp. 97, 105).

Earlier in his essay Engels asks whether it is "possible to have organisation without authority." Supposing, he said, "a social revolution dethroned the capitalists ... that the land and the instruments of labour had become the collective property of the workers ... particular questions arise ... concerning the mode of production, distribution of materials, etc., which must be settled at once ...; whether they are settled by decision of a delegate ... or, if possible, by a majority vote, the will of the single individual will always have to subordinate itself, which means that questions are settled in an authoritarian way. ... We have thus seen that, on the one hand, a certain authority, no matter how delegated, and, on the other hand, a certain subordination, are things which independently of all social organisation, are imposed upon us ... ." (in *Anarchism and Anarcho-Syndicalism*, 1974, pp. 103-4). Marx, also, in Volume 1 of *Capital*, says that "All combined labour on a large scale requires, more or less, a directing authority, in order to secure the harmonious working of the individual activities, ..." (1983, Part IV, Chap. XIII, p. 313).

Thus, even in communist society "a certain authority" and "a certain subordination" would continue to exist. Marx and Engels assumed that this would not lead to new forms of domination and envisaged communism as a society in which, as described by Engels, "the interests of individuals are not opposed to one another", the "public interest is no longer distinct from that of each individual," and "the interests of all coincide". But, as Selucký says, Marx's assertion that "there will be no room for domination is not adequately substantiated. For a long period of time ... all persons elected to general functions will administer not only things but also people. And whoever adminsters people, or decides about people, is in a dominant position vis-à-vis those who are the objects of his decisions."

In a memorandum on "The Nationalisation of the Land" written and published in 1872 (Marx-Engels, *Selected Works* in three volumes, Vol. 2 (1977) p. 290) Marx writes: "There will be no longer any government or state power, distinct from society itself! ... *National centralisation of the means of production* will become the national basis of a society composed of associations of free and equal producers, carrying on the social business on a common and rational plan. ..." Such a plan, Marx assumes, "maintains the proper proportion between the different kinds of work to be done and the various wants of the community." (*Capital*, Vol. 1, Chap. 1, Section 4, 1983, p. 83).

As Nove shows, however, Marx "never considered the organisational implications of his ideas." The "view that production relations and plans would be 'simple' and 'transparent', that the interests of society would be defined and perceived, was very seriously mistaken." In a complex modern economy, with its scale and specialisation, "the elimination of commodity production, with production for use and not for exchange, implies a degree of centralisation ... a multilevel, hierarchically organised plan-bureaucracy" which "conflicts with the aim of meaningful workers' participation in decision-making at their place of work. Marx's notions on the overcoming of 'horizontal' and 'vertical' division of labour are wide of any possible application in practice. He left contradictory indications on the need for one directing will *and* on decisions by freely associating producers. ..."

"What Marx did, in effect," says Timothy McCarthy, "was to engraft upon the industrial working class of early capitalism a set of goals and aspirations which were derived not from an observation of its actual attitudes and behaviour, but from the speculative conception of man elaborated in the early writings. ... Marxism presents itself as a rigorously scientific theory of society standing in need of no a priori assumptions; however, its central doctrine - the revolutionary mission of the proletariat - was derived in a priori fashion from a purely speculative doctrine of 'human essence,' which resists empirical verification." (*Marx and the Proletariat: A Study in Social Theory,* 1978, p. 69). Peter Singer, in his assessment of Marx's thought, concludes by quoting and commenting on a section of Marx's notes on Bakunin's *Statism and Anarchy.* "The tragedy of Marxism", Singer says, is that our experience "bears out Bakunin's objections rather than Marx's replies."

The "Dictator" of the International

The International Working Men's Association, subsequently known as the First International, was founded in September 1864. Marx put forward an "Address and Provisional Rules" of the Working Men's International Association, written in English, which was adopted and published in November 1864. This came to be known as the "Inaugural Address" as though Marx had delivered it at the inaugural meeting of the International. The Address, said Engels, "could not at once proclaim the principles laid down in the [*Communist*] *Manifesto,* it was bound to be broad enough to be acceptable to all parties". (55) But as Marx pointed out in a letter to Engels (11 September, 1867) cited by Schwarzschild (p.271): "... in the next revolution, which is perhaps nearer than it appears, *we* (i.e. you and I) will have this powerful engine *in our hands*". (56)

Writing to Dr. Kugelmann on 28 March, 1870, Marx enclosed a letter of "Confidential Information - not intended for the public" which gave the text of a circular written by Marx and issued by the General Council of the International Working Men's Association, London, on 16 January, 1870. Referring to the question of the formation of a regional Council for England, the circular said: "... The General Council being at present placed in the happy position of having its hand directly on this great lever of the proletarian revolution, it would be sheer folly, ... almost ... an outright crime, to allow that hold to fall into purely English hands. The English have all the material requisites necessary for the social revolution. What they lack is the spirit of generalisation and revolutionary ardour. It is only the General Council which can supply this deficiency, which can thus accelerate the truly revolutionary movement in this country and consequently everywhere. ... As the General Council we can initiate measures ... which later, in the public execution of their tasks, appear as spontaneous movements of the English working class." (57)

In the "Inaugural Address" Marx asserted that "the misery of the working masses has not diminished from 1848 to 1864 ... Everywhere the great mass of the working classes were sinking down to a lower depth, at the same rate at least that those above them were rising in the social scale". To buttress this assertion, David Felix says: "Marx inserted in his logic" a "lie which is repeated every time the Address is reprinted." He craftily isolated and quoted part of a sentence attributed to William Gladstone, then Chancellor of the British Exchequer, in his budget speech of 1863: " 'This intoxicating augmentation of wealth and power', adds Mr. Gladstone, 'is entirely confined to classes of property' ". This, however, perverted and contradicted the sense of what Gladstone had said (as reported in some seven London newspapers on April 17, 1863) which was: "I should look almost with apprehension and with pain upon this intoxicating augmentation of wealth and power if it were my belief that it was confined to the classes who are in easy circumstances". Gladstone went on to say that "the average condition of the British labourer, we have the happiness to know, has improved during the last twenty years in a degree which we know to be extraordinary, and which we may almost pronounce to be unexampled in the history of any country and of any age". ("The Times", April 17, 1863; the report in "The Morning Star" of April 17, 1863, reads similarly).

The falsification, says Felix, "also appeared in *Das Kapital* but with new discrepancies". The text of recent English-language editions of Volume 1 of *Capital* (Chapter XXV) includes the words "Morning Star, April 17" as the source for Marx's statement. Marx's truncated and altered version can, however, be compared with the text of the report of Gladstone's speech in "The Morning Star" (and other newspapers) - see pages 181-183 of Volume 22 (1963) of the Marx-Engels *Werke.*

David Felix outlines and reviews the whole course of the controversy which this matter aroused and which engaged Marx, his daughter Eleanor, and Engels in a series of debates over a period of some twenty years. The conclusions at which he arrives in *Marx As Politician* (1983) (58) are precisely the same as those reached by Chushichi Tsuzuki in a book published 16 years earlier which is not included in Felix's Bibliography. In *The Life of Eleanor Marx, 1855-1898, A Socialist Tragedy* (1967, p.110), Tsuzuki writes: "In the 'Inaugural Address' of the International Working Men's Association, Gladstone was made to have said that the growth of wealth in the fifties had been confined to classes of property, but this was exactly opposite to what he actually meant". Raddatz refers to research showing that in other instances (e.g. Adam Smith) Marx did not copy out or translate correctly passages which he extracted. (59)

In the spring of 1865, Marx wrote to Engels: "Apart from my work on the book, the *International Association* takes up a quite enormous amount of time, because I am in fact its head. And what a waste of time it is! ... Take this French shit, for example: ...". (60) In a reference to Marx, the German Social Democratic leader, August Bebel, in his *Reminiscences* says: "Thus wrote the 'dictator' of the International." (61) Marx himself, in Volume III (Chapter XXIII) of *Capital,* declared that: "All labour in which many individuals co-operate necessarily requires a commanding will to co-ordinate and unify the process, ...". (62) In a letter to Engels (25 August 1851) Marx wrote of "a communist's pride in infallibility". (*Collected*

Works, Vol. 38, p. 440). And in the Manifesto of the Communist Party (February, 1848), despite references to the "immense majority", special trust is put in the charismatic few who have the "advantage" over the "great mass" of "clearly understanding the line of march." (Marx-Engels, *Collected Works,* Vol. 6, pp. 494-95, 497).

As Engels disclosed in 1884 in an article on "Marx and the Neue Rheinische Zeitung": "On the outbreak of the February Revolution [in 1848], the German Communist Party, as we called it, consisted only of a small corps, the Communist League, which was organised as a secret propaganda society." In the *Manifesto* Marx established the Communists as "on the one hand, practically, the most advanced and resolute section of the working-class parties of every country, that section which pushes forward all others; on the other hand, theoretically, they have over the great mass of the proletariat the advantage of clearly understanding the line of march, the conditions and the ultimate general results of the proletarian movement". In that one sentence, says David Felix, Marx "gave his party the exclusive leadership over the proletariat and the future. It was sleight of hand of the highest order: he had identified a political party with a social class and then, by attributing superior understanding to the party, confided to it the function of thinking and acting for that class." As for the other parties, in a private letter of December 18, 1889, Engels indicated that the proletarian party can "for a short time make use of other parties for its aims," adding that: "You will find this policy expounded as early as 1847 in *The Communist Manifesto* and we followed it in 1848, in the International and throughout." (Karl Marx, *Selected Works* in two volumes, Vol. II, London, 1933, pp. 28-9; David Felix, *Marx As Politician,* 1983, pp. 77-8).

The first congress of the International was held in Geneva in September 1866. Marx drew up detailed "Instructions" for the delegates of the Provisional General Council to the congress. In these "Instructions", written in English in August 1866 and published February/March, 1867, Marx said: "In a rational state of society *every child whatever,* from the age of 9 years, ought to become a productive labourer in the same way that no able-bodied adult person ought to be exempted from the general law of nature, viz.: to work in order to be able to eat, and work not only with the brain but with the hands too". In his "Marginal Notes to the Programme of the German Workers' Party" (1875) - which came to be known as the *Critique of the Gotha Programme* - Marx's comments on the "Prohibition of child labour" were: "... A general prohibition of child labour is incompatible with the existence of large-scale industry and hence an empty, pious wish. Its realization - if it were possible - would be reactionary, ...". (63) The obscurities and defects in Marx's *Critique* are analysed in Alec Nove's recent evaluation of the relevance of Marxism to contemporary social and economic problems. (64)

At a congress of the International held at The Hague in 1872 it was decided, in view of increasing divisions and disputes, to transfer the General Council to New York. "The Hague Congress", said Engels (cited by Schwarzschild), "was really the end" of the First International. A day after the congress, on September 8, 1872, at Amsterdam, Marx made what Robert Payne says was "his last public speech". According to what is stated to be "the most accurate report" of the speech, Marx declared: "... we do not deny that there are countries, such as America and England, and if I was familiar with its institutions, I might include Holland, where the workers may attain their goal by peaceful means." But this statement, in the conditional mood, was not the end of Marx's speech. In the next sentence he continued, "That being the case, we must recognize that in most continental countries the lever of the revolution will have to be force: a resort to force will be necessary one day in order to set up the rule of labour." (65)

Marx and the Ideology of Fascism

Contained in A. James Gregor's remarkable books *The Ideology of Fascism* (1969) and *Contemporary Radical Ideologies* (1968), and other writings, is a close analysis of arguments tendered by Marx himself and a wealth of documentation showing that both Marxism and Fascism are rooted in the same ideological traditions and share some essential features and critical convictions. This is revealed in the similarity of the arguments advanced in their support.

"Recent philosophy", Marx wrote in 1842 (*Collected Works,* Vol. 1, p. 202), "proceeds from the idea of the whole. It looks on the state as the great organism, in which legal, moral, and political freedom must be realised, and in which the individual citizen in obeying the laws of the state only obeys the natural laws of his own reason, of human reason."

In Marx's *Economic and Philosophical Manuscripts* (1959, pp. 104 ff.) the relationship between the individual and "social being" is regularly reduced to one of identity. "The individual *is the social being*. His life ... is therefore ... an expression and confirmation of *social life*. Man's individual and species life are not *different* ... Man, much as he may therefore be a *particular* individual ... is just as much the *totality* - ... ."

For Marx, "man" *is* "the human world, the state, society". ("Toward The Critique Of Hegel's Philosophy Of Law: Introduction"). And as Professor Selucký writes (*Marxism, Socialism, Freedom*, 1979, p. 77): "In one of his key works ["Theses on Feuerbach"] Marx even dehumanised man by saying that 'the human essence is no abstraction inherent in each single individual. In its reality, it is the ensemble of the social relations'." Or as J. Middleton Murry put it in *Marxism* (John Wiley and Sons, 1935, p. 15): "My concrete individuality - in Marx's outstanding phrase - is 'the totality of social relations': ... I am dissolved into the social whole."

In *Capital* Marx wrote: "... individuals are dealt with only insofar as they are the personifications of economic categories, embodiments of particular class relations and class interests. My standpoint, ... can less than any other make the individual responsible for relations whose creature he socially remains. ... the capitalist is merely capital personified ... ." (Vol. 1, 1983, pp. 20-1; Vol. III, 1984, p. 819).

"Marx's arguments," says Gregor, "are curiously Hegelian in character and implication, and the 'individuality', 'fulfilment' and 'freedom' promised are Hegelian 'individuality', 'fulfilment', and 'freedom', *the unity of the particular with the universal.*" Freedom is not "understood to mean freedom from constraint; it means behaviour in conformity to law". By identifying the individual with a "totality" (whether it be society or the state) which is understood to constitute the human "essence", any "real distinction between freedom and constraint, between private and public interest", is removed and it can be argued that "the interests of the 'totality' and the individual must ultimately coincide." As stated by Engels: "In communist society, where the interests of individuals are not opposed to one another but, on the contrary, are united, ... the public interest is no longer distinct from that of each individual! ... the interests of all coincide, ..." ("Speeches in Elberfeld," *Collected Works*, Vol. 4, pp. 246, 249).

Gregor adds that Lenin, in the tradition of classical Marxism and under the direct influence of Hegel, argued such an identity between collective and individual interests with the claim that: "the *individual is* the universal. ... Consequently the opposites (the individual is opposed to the universal) are identical ... Every individual is (in one way or another) a universal." (*Collected Works,* Vol. 38, 1972, p. 361).

As Gregor demonstrates, essentially the same arguments are fundamental to the political and social philosophy of Giovanni Gentile, the principal intellectual apologist of Mussolini's Fascism and the author of the philosophic part of its official ideology. Gentile's affinities with classical Marxism in this respect have not gone unnoticed, Gregor says, and the similarities of argument have a common origin "in the Hegelianism which is their ultimate historic source." In his last work, *Genesis and Structure of Society* (1966. Translated by H.S. Harris from the edition of 1946. Pp. 85-6, 89, 98-9), Gentile writes: "To sum up then: in the individual, particularity and universality coincide. The more he is himself the more closely he is identified with all men. ... So the real individual is not opposed to the universal - he *is* the universal. ... the immanence of community in the individual becomes manifest. ... The human individual is not an atom. Immanent in the concept of an individual is the concept of society. ... for the synthesis involves opposition, but it involves also the *identity* of the opposites." (See also A. James Gregor, *Contemporary Radical Ideologies,* pp. 39-40, 46, 50; *The Ideology of Fascism,* pp. 333-4, 337, 340, 342, 344-5; "Classical Marxism and the Totalitarian Ethic" in *Value Theory in Philosophy and Social Science,* Edited by Ervin Laszlo and James B. Wilbur, 1973, pp. 146-7, 151-2).

In *A Dictionary of Marxist Thought* (1985, p. 147), Steven Lukes, in criticising aspects of Marx's view of freedom - and that of later Marxists who have followed him in these respects - observes that: "Such formulations are theoretically in error and have been practically disastrous. ... In practice the failure to call liberal freedoms freedom has legitimized their wholesale suppression and denial, all too often in the name of freedom itself."

"If it were my aim to write a history of the rise of totalitarianism," says Karl Popper, "I should have to deal with Marxism first; for fascism grew partly out of the spiritual and political breakdown of Marxism. ...

Hegel's identity philosophy, by contributing to historicism and to an identification of might and right, encouraged totalitarian modes of thought." (*The Open Society And Its Enemies,* Vol. II, 1969, pp. 60, 395).

Future Society, Crime and Punishment

In *Marx and History* (University of Texas Press, 1979) in a section on "The Future Society" (p. 90), D. Ross Gandy writes: "Nor will people resort to violence in social conflicts. In communist society, says Marx, there will be no more revolutions, only social evolution. Conflict results in argument, discussion, and debate, and people settle their differences by a vote. ... What about personal conflicts? Will there be crimes of passion, like murder? No, only class society, based on exploitation and violence, breeds murderers."

Gandy cites the Marx-Engels *Werke* (4:182 and 8: 506-509) as the source of these assertions. These references are to Marx's book *The Poverty of Philosophy* (*Collected Works,* Vol. 6, p. 212) and his article on "Capital Punishment" (*Collected Works,* Vol. 11, pp. 495-498). Gandy also cites Engels (*Werke,* 2:542) i.e. his "Speech in Elberfeld". (*Collected Works,* Vol. 4, pp. 248-249).

"Communism", wrote Marx, "is the position as the negation of the negation". It "already knows itself" to be "the transcendence of human self-estrangement". It is "the *genuine* resolution of the conflict between man and nature and between man and man". (*Economic and Philosophic Manuscripts,* 1959, pp. 101-2, 114). Marx refers to "the teaching of materialism on the original goodness and equal intellectual endowment of men" and says "how necessarily materialism is connected with communism and socialism" and, in a discussion of crime and punishment, he looks to a condition of society in which "under *human* conditions punishment will *really* be nothing but the sentence passed by the culprit on himself". (*The Holy Family,* Marx-Engels, *Collected Works,* Vol. 4, pp. 130, 179). This view of punishment which will *really* "make the criminal the 'judge' of his 'own' crime" was derived by Marx from a critical examination of a formula given by Hegel in *The Philosophy of Right.* As quoted by Marx, Hegel says that "Punishment is the *right* of the criminal. ... His crime is the negation of right. Punishment is the negation of this negation, and consequently an affirmation of right, solicited and forced upon the criminal by himself ". (*The Holy Family, Collected Works*, Vol. 4, pp. 178-9; "Capital Punishment", *Collected Works*, Vol. 11, pp. 496-7).

Again, in an article of 1853 on "The Indian Question - Irish Tenant Right" Marx writes: "Legislature, magistracy and armed force, are all of them but the offspring of improper conditions of society, preventing those arrangements among men which would make useless the compulsory intervention of a third supreme power". (Marx and Engels, *Ireland and the Irish Question*, Moscow, 1971, p. 61). The implications of this sentence are intriguing, says Paul Phillips (*Marx and Engels on Law and Laws*, 1980, p. 189): "The suggestion that some arrangements among men would 'make useless the compulsory intervention of a third supreme power' contains by implication a whole view of human nature. The view implied is the same as that necessary to make the 'withering away of Law and State' a credible possibility, namely that everyone is by nature a social being and that it is only the arrangements of society that induce anti-social behaviour. This view, like any view of what people are 'basically' like (i.e. abstracting from the empirical human situation), is of course a value judgement".

In "A Note on Utopia", Appendix 3 to *The Economics of Feasible Socialism* (1983), Alec Nove says that "The terms 'utopia' and 'utopian' have been used pejoratively here, and applied to Marx's vision of socialism and to the ideas of some 'new leftists'. ... As argued already, while of course recognising the role and desirability of ideals, some of these utopian notions create dangerous illusion, confuse the mind. Let me illustrate with an example. A society without crime is a noble and worthy aim, and we should indeed strive to eliminate crime, and to look at data on murder, rape and burglary as deplorable instances of failure measured against the proper ideal - unattainable but the goal - which is constituted by their absence (and so long as they exist, no one would assert that we do without police, locksmiths, etc). However, the notion of society without conflict, in which (to cite Agnes Heller again) 'every individual strives for the same thing ... every individual expresses the needs of all other individuals and it cannot be otherwise,' is impossible (and even undesirable), in my view, and anyone holding such a belief about socialism is bound to be misled, and *dangerously* misled." The reference is to Agnes Heller's book *The Theory of Need in Marx*, 1976, p. 125.

Engels, in "Speeches in Elberfeld" (Marx-Engels, *Collected Works*, Vol. 4, pp. 248-249), declares that "In communist society ... We eliminate the contradiction between the individual man and all others, we counterpose social peace to social war, we put the axe to the *root* of crime - ... Crimes against property cease of their own accord where everyone receives what he needs to satisfy his natural and his spiritual urges, where social gradations and distinctions cease to exist. Justice concerned with criminal cases ceases of itself, that dealing with civil cases, ... likewise disappears; conflicts can then be only rare exceptions, ... and will be easily settled by arbitrators ... in a society in which community of interests has become the basic principle, and in which the public interest is no longer distinct from that of each individual! ... where the interests of all coincide,... ." As the Polish writer W. Bienkowski remarks in *Theory and Reality* (1981, p. 96): "Nearly all utopias, no matter how scientifically based, in their depiction of the future are unconscious dreams of a return to paradise... All of them aim, in one way or the other, to 'put an end' to history, to plunge its processes again into an organic fusion of the individual and society".

Engels's book *The Condition of the Working-Class in England* was described by a contemporary reviewer as "a call for murder and arson written with bile, blood and passion". According to Terrell Carver it "was biased and politically partial" and "Engels's use of sources was highly selective". (*Engels*, 1981, p. 14). In the Appendix to the American edition (1887), which was included in the Preface to the English and German editions of 1892, Engels acknowledged that "this book exhibits everywhere the traces of the descent of modern Socialism from one of its ancestors - German philosophy".

In his book, Engels wrote:- "...This reserve army,...is the 'surplus population' of England,... When these people find no work and will not rebel against society, what remains for them but to beg? ... And he among the 'surplus' who has courage and passion enough openly to resist society, to reply with declared war upon the bourgeoisie to the disguised war which the bourgeoisie wages upon him, goes forth to rob, plunder, murder, and burn! ... He is poor, life offers him no charm, almost every enjoyment is denied him, the penalties of the law have no further terrors for him; why should he restrain his desires, why leave to the rich the enjoyment of his birthright, why not seize a part of it for himself? ... He is the passive subject of all possible combinations of circumstances, ... Either he seeks to keep his head above water in this whirlpool, to rescue his manhood, and this he can do solely in rebellion against the class which plunders him so mercilessly and then abandons him to his fate, ... or he gives up the struggle against his fate as hopeless,... Once more the worker must choose, must either surrender himself to his fate, become a 'good' workman, heed 'faithfully' the interest of the bourgeoisie, in which case he most certainly becomes a brute, or else he must rebel, fight for his manhood to the last, and this he can only do in the fight against the bourgeoisie. ...

The contempt for the existing social order is most conspicuous in its extreme form - that of offences against the law. If the influences demoralising to the working-man act more powerfully, more concentratedly than usual, he becomes an offender as certainly as water abandons the fluid for the vaporous state at 80 degrees, Réamur. Under the brutal and brutalising treatment of the bourgeoisie, the working-man becomes precisely as much a thing without volition as water, and is subject to the laws of Nature with precisely the same necessity; ... In this country, social war is under full headway, ... And this war grows from year to year, as the criminal tables show, more violent, passionate, irreconcilable. The enemies are dividing gradually into two great camps - the bourgeoisie on the one hand, the workers on the other. ... it may very well surprise us that the bourgeoisie remains so quiet and composed in the face of the rapidly gathering storm-clouds, that it can read all these things daily in the papers without, we will not say indignation at such a social condition, but fear of its consequences, of a universal outburst of that which manifests itself symptomatically from day to day in the form of crime. ... I think the people will not endure more than one more crisis. ... If, up to that time, the English bourgeoisie does not pause to reflect - and to all appearance it certainly will not do so - a revolution will follow with which none hitherto known can be compared. ... the vengeance of the people will come down with a wrath of which the rage of 1793 gives no true idea. ... this I maintain, the war of the poor against the rich now carried on in detail and indirectly will become direct and universal. It is too late for a peaceful solution." (Marx-Engels, *Collected Works,* Vol. 4, pp. 384-86, 412-13, 416, 425, 427, 581-83, 701-02).

In a recent book, *The Idea of Poverty : England in the Early Industrial Age* (1984, p. 287), Gertrude Himmelfarb refers to "the powerful ideology Engels imposed on the actuality of history". And she adds that "If the English working classes never carried out Engels's prediction of revolution, it was for the same reason that they resisted the label 'proletariat' - resisted in fact the whole of the historical schema that would have made them what Lenin was pleased to call a 'fighting proletariat' ".

In *Crime and Capitalism : Readings in Marxist Criminology* (ed. David F. Greenberg, Mayfield Publishing Company, 1981) it is stated (p. 414) that "some Marxian criminologists have argued that crime does serve progressive functions in a capitalist society. Some see it, as Engels did in *The Condition of the Working Class in England*, as the first stage in the development of a socialist consciousness. ... Capitalism generates ever-increasing levels of crime, forcing the state to spend more and more revenue on crime control. Crime thus contributes to the fiscal crisis of the state." And reference is made to "the position that crime advances the socialist revolution, ...".

On page 415 it is said that "The broader participation in radical social movements of recent years (from students, women, prisoners, and homosexuals) suggests a less restrictive notion of how revolutions are made." There is a reference on the same page to "ex-mental patients". According to Richard Quinney (1974), as reported on page 421, "criminals are in some sense rebels against bourgeois society, and thus constitute a potentially revolutionary class".

Elsewhere in the book it is suggested that it was a problem of theft that first forced Marx to realize his ignorance of political economy and that class struggle first presented itself to Marx's serious attention as a form of crime. It is pointed out that "Marx's preoccupation with revolutionary political movements grew out of his attempts to grapple with the philosophical legacy of Hegel". (pp. 78, 484).

Maximilien Rubel, author of the standard bibliography, in French, of Marx's writings, in *Rubel on Karl Marx : Five Essays* (Cambridge, 1981, p. 28) says that "In a sense Marx is the most utopian of the utopians". In *The German Ideology* Marx and Engels declare that "In communist society, where nobody has one exclusive sphere of activity but each can become accomplished in any branch he wishes, society regulates the general production and thus makes it possible for me to do one thing today and another tomorrow, to hunt in the morning, fish in the afternoon, rear cattle in the evening, criticise after dinner, just as I have a mind, without ever becoming hunter, fisherman, shepherd or critic." (*Collected Works,* Vol. 5, p. 47).

Nove comments on this "singularly ill-chosen" formulation in a section of his recent book (op.cit., 1983, pp. 46-50) on the "Division of Labour". As he remarks, "Most labour is social labour in the sense that each contributes to joint endeavours which would be disrupted if someone freely chose to go fishing instead".

From the similarity of views pointed out by Professor H.B. Acton in *The Illusion Of The Epoch* (1962, pp. 235-36), it would seem that Marx and Engels derived their account of communist society in *The German Ideology* from the French utopian socialist François Fourier. In one of Fourier's accounts of what he called "attractive labour" he describes a day in the life of a member of the future society as consisting of "attendance at the hunting group", "attendance at the fishing group", "attendance at the agricultural group under cover", and attendance at four or five other groups, as well as work in the library, visits to the "court of the arts, ball, theatre, receptions," etc. And in *The Holy Family* Marx refers to "Fourier's assertion that the right to fish, to hunt, etc., are inborn rights of men". (Marx-Engels, *Collected Works,* Vol. 4, p. 88).

In *Principles of Communism* (Marx-Engels, *Collected Works,* Vol. 6, pp. 341-357), Engels says that as a result of the abolition of private property and the communist organisation of society "the division of labour making one man a peasant, another a shoemaker, a third a factory worker, a fourth a stockjobber, which has already been undermined by machines, will completely disappear. Education will enable young people quickly to go through the whole system of production, it will enable them to pass from one branch of industry to another according to the needs of society or their own inclinations". With this, there will be "the complete annihilation of classes and their antagonisms".

Marx, in *Capital* Vol. 1 (Part IV, Chap. XV, Section 9, 1977, p. 458), and Engels, in *Anti-Dühring* (first published in 1877-78, Part III, Chap. III), refer to the "abolition of the old division of labour". In

Anti-Dühring, the "whole manuscript" of which, says Engels (in the Preface of 1885 to the second German edition), was read to Marx "before it was printed", Engels confidently promises that: "In time to come there will no longer be any professional porters or architects, and the man who for half an hour gives instructions as an architect will also act as a porter for a period, until his activity as an architect is once again required." (loc.cit., Part II, Chap. VI, 1977, pp. 243-44).

In "Speeches in Elberfeld" Engels asserts that "In communist society it will be easy to be informed about both production and consumption. Since we know how much, on the average, a person needs, it is easy to calculate how much is needed by a given number of individuals, and since production is no longer in the hands of private producers, but in those of the community and its administrative bodies, it is a trifling matter *to regulate production according to needs*". (Marx-Engels, *Collected Works,* Vol. 4, p. 246). And in *Capital* Marx says that in "a community of free individuals, carrying on their work with the means of production in common, ... the labour-power of all the different individuals is consciously applied as the combined labour-power of the community. All the characteristics of Robinson's [i.e. Robinson Crusoe's] labour are here repeated, but with this difference, that they are social, instead of individual. ... The social relations of the individual producers, with regard both to their labour and to its products, are in this case perfectly simple and intelligible, and that with regard not only to production but also to distribution." (Vol. 1, Part 1, Chap. 1, Section 4, 1977, pp. 82-3). In *Anti-Dühring,* Part III Socialism, Engels writes: "From the moment when society enters into possession of the means of production and uses them in direct association for production, the labour of each individual, however varied its specifically useful character may be, becomes at the start and directly social labour. ... People will be able to manage everything very simply, ... ". (Chap. IV., 1977, pp. 374-75).

Again, in a Circular from the General Council of the International, in 1872, Marx and Engels declare that "once the aim of the proletarian movement, the abolition of classes has been attained, the power of the State, which serves to keep the great majority of producers under the yoke of a numerically small exploiting minority, disappears, and the functions of government are transformed into simple administrative functions". And shortly afterwards, Engels reiterates that: "All Socialists are agreed that the political state, and with it political authority, will disappear as a result of the coming social revolution, that is, that public functions will lose their political character and be transformed into the simple administrative functions of watching over the true interests of society." (Marx-Engels, *Selected Works* in three volumes, Vol. Two, Moscow, 1973, pp. 285, 378).

As Aron Katsenellenboigen (cited by Nove, op.cit., 1983, p. 33) remarks of the authors of such writings: they were "romantics on this issue... The classical scholars of Marxism conceived of future society as a system in which everything would be obvious. People's goals would be obvious, as would the available resources for transforming them into products needed by the population ...". Nove (pp. 39f., 59f.) critically examines Marx's gross underestimation of the complexity of the modern economy and society and his concept of a future society which "is as unreal as is Marx's parallel with Robinson Crusoe (or a patriarchal family unit, another of the parallels used by Marx)."

In "Marx's Vision of Communism: A Reconstruction" (in *Critique* 8, Summer 1977, pp. 4-41) Bertell Ollman offers what is said to be "the fullest reconstruction of Marx's views of the future available in English". Ollman presents a detailed retrieval of "descriptions of the future society [are] scattered throughout Marx's writings ... from his writings of 1844 - the year in which he set down the broad lines of his analysis - to the end of his life".

In this article Ollman reconstructs Marx's projections for the first stage of the communist future and the second stage or "full communism". In *Critique of the Gotha Programme*, in discussing "the co-operative society based on common ownership of the means of production", Marx refers to "the first phase of communist society" and "a higher phase of communist society". Lenin, however, in *State and Revolution* (1917) inserted the words "(usually called socialism)" after "the first phase of communist society". Lenin, says Stanley Moore, revised prevailing terminology and renamed socialism what Marx calls the first stage of communism. The contrast which Lenin drew between socialism and communism then became, in Tom Bottomore's words, "part of Leninist orthodoxy". (Stanley Moore, *Marx on the Choice between Socialism and Communism*, 1980, pp. 1, 3; Tom Bottomore, in *A Dictionary of Marxist Thought*, 1985, p. 89).

Ollman claims that he has "not gone beyond Marx's actual words in piecing together the components of the communist society". Features of Marx's vision of communism, as detailed by Ollman, include the following:-

Factories, machines, skills, etc., have been provided "in abundance" by capitalism, says Ollman, and in the first stage of communism the wealth which capitalism left is "multiplied many times over". Wide-scale planning has been enormously successful. Technology has developed to a plane where practically anything is possible.

In the only instance where figures are given, Ollman says, it appears that the revolution will cut each worker's day in half but society will produce more than before. The reference here is to Marx's *Theories of Surplus Value,* Part III, [Chapter XXI], Section 1., Moscow, 1975, p. 256.

Marx, adds Ollman, "never doubts that his proletarian planners - whose actual planning mechanisms are never discussed - will make the right equations". The general costs of administration not belonging to production will, however, be very considerably restricted in comparison with present-day society.

Instead of money, in this first stage of communism, what we have are pieces of paper (certificates, vouchers) which state how much labour-time each worker has contributed (less a deduction for the common fund). These entitle the holder to draw from the social stock of consumption goods as much as costs the same amount of labour. In Volume II of *Capital* (Part III, Chapter XVIII, Section II, 1974, p. 362) Marx says: "These vouchers are not money. They do not circulate". Ollman adds that "Such limitations on the power and function of wage payments puts an end to the money system as we know it".

In the wake of the proletarian revolution there will be "the democratic rule of the entire working class". Ollman quotes Marx as explaining that: "as long as other classes, especially the capitalist class, still exist, as long as the proletariat is still struggling with it ... it must use coercive means, hence governmental means; it is still a class, and the economic conditions on which the class-struggle and the existence of classes rest, have not yet disappeared and must be removed by force, or transformed, their process of transformation must be speeded up by force". This is quoted from Marx's "Conspectus of Bakunin's Book *State and Anarchy*" (1874-75).

Marx believed, says Ollman, that under proletarian rule people in the government do not have important interests which conflict with those of the class from which they come and will want to represent the workers correctly. Should the electors make a "mistake" it will be quickly rectified through the instrument of the recall. To believe that workers elected to government will use their authority to advance personal ends is, as Marx puts it, to have "nightmares about authority".

Ollman admits that Marx's picture of life and organisation in the first stage of communism is very incomplete; that we can only guess how much power workers enjoy in their enterprises and through what mechanisms they exercise it; that not much is said about how conflicts between individuals or between groups are resolved, and so on.

In *Critique of the Gotha Programme* Marx speaks of "defects" which are "inevitable in the first phase of communist society". Thus, "one man is superior to another physically or mentally and so supplies more labour in the same time, or can labour for a longer time". Tacit recognition is therefore given to "unequal individual endowment and thus productive capacity as natural privileges". Further, "one worker is married, another is not; one has more children than another and so on and so forth. Thus ... one will be richer than another, and so on."

But, says Ollman, with the completion of the various aspects of life and organization associated with the first stage of communism, the second stage starts on its way with "a super abundance of all material goods". The community stores are "replete with everything a communist person could possibly want" and "everyone can have as much of anything as he wants". According to Marx, "the enslaving subordination of individuals under division of labour, and therewith also the antithesis between mental and physical labour, has vanished, after labour has become not merely a means to live but has become itself the primary necessity of life, after the productive forces have also increased with the all-round development of the individual, and all the springs of co-operative wealth flow more abundantly". The limitations of the first phase of communism can then be wholly left behind and society can apply the rule: "From each according to his ability, to each according to his needs".

Thus, "the division of labour, as Marx understands it, has come to an end". Social ownership has been extended and private property abolished. In one place Marx speaks of communism as "the *positive* transcendence of *private property*".

"When class rule has disappeared", declares Marx, "a state in the now accepted political sense of the word no longer exists". ("The Conspectus of Bakunin's Book *State and Anarchy*"). And in *The Holy Family* (Chapter VIII) Marx writes: "... *punishment, coercion,* is contrary to *human* conduct ... under *human* conditions ... the culprit ... will see in *other* men his natural saviours from the punishment which he has imposed on himself." (*Collected Works,* Vol. 4, p. 179). In *Socialism: Utopian and Scientific,* first published in French in 1880, Engels says that: "The interference of the state power in social relations becomes superfluous in one sphere after another, and then dies away of itself. The government of persons is replaced by the administration of things and the direction of the processes of production. The state is not 'abolished', *it withers away.*" (Chapter III, Peking, 1975, p.94. In *Anti-Dühring,* Moscow, 1947 reprinted 1977, p. 341, which is stated to be "reproduced from the authorised English translation" of *Socialism : Utopian and Scientific,* the last three words read: *"It dies out"*).

"People's activities," says Ollman, "are no longer organized by external forces, with the exception of productive work where such organization still exists ... . As a part of this, restrictive rules are unknown; nor is there any coercion or punishment". Referring to "the discipline enforced by the capitalist for combined labour" Marx says that "This discipline will become superfluous under a social system in which the labourers work for their own account." (*Capital,* Vol. III, Part 1, Chap. V, Section I., 1977, p. 83). Marx recognised the need for "a directing authority" in the communist production process but drew an analogy between this and the authority relation which he took to exist between a conductor and an orchestra. (*Capital,* Vol. 1, Part IV, Chap. XIII, 1977, p. 313; Vol. III, Part V, Chap. XXIII, 1977, p. 383). Ollman does not mention the comments made by Michael Evans on this: "Assuming agreement on what to play, there are often considerable disagreements between the conductor and the members of the orchestra about the interpretation of the music. And in no society of any complexity has it ever been the case that everyone has wanted to play the same tune". (*Karl Marx,* 1975, p. 163).

Marx appreciated the need for authority and according to Engels ("On Authority," 1872-3) "the will of the single individual will always have to subordinate itself ". And "if this is true with respect to the individual", comments A. James Gregor, "how much more so would it be with respect to the locally organized communes which must be integrated into the single vast plan which is to govern" communist society? "It is difficult to imagine how a single vast plan of social production could be organized and administered by delegates possessed of only a short-term mandate (always subject to recall) and bound by explicit instructions". (*A Survey of Marxism,* p. 200). Marx "gave no hint", says Evans, as to how a balance would be organised and maintained between those central functions formerly undertaken by the state and "a system of local and regional communes" to which "a range of (unspecified) functions would devolve". (*Karl Marx,* pp. 152, 157). As Nove points out: "The task of ensuring integration and co-ordination - the task of planning - is a difficult and responsible one. It is unlikely that anyone can just take his or her turn in doing it", in between, say, "driving heavy lorries and filling teeth." The trouble with Marx's notions on overcoming the division of labour is that "he does *not* say that people should be able to change their specialisation, but that there would be no specialisation at all". (op.cit., 1983, pp. 47-8).

Despite these evident difficulties, Ollman continues with his recon-struction of Marx's vision of communism. The work of administration, more properly of coordination, is, he says, the only function in communism which is analogous to the duties of a modern state, and Marx believed that communism as a complex industrial society could be run effectively in this manner. There would be new aims and standards, and, above all, "new communist people". Communism is "a society which knows no clash of basic interests" and is "unique in having administrators and administered who are striving to achieve the same ends." For Marx, "the fate of all final forms of parliamentarism" is "that of being ranged under the category of nuisances". ("The Indian Question", in *Karl Marx on Colonialism and Modernization,* ed. Shlomo Avineri, 1969, p. 200).

In the second stage of communism, Ollman writes (p. 22): "The divisions we are accustomed to seeing in the human species along lines of nation, race, religion, geographical section (town dweller and country dweller), occupation, class, and family have all ceased to exist."

With regard to the family, in the original text of the "Theses on Feuerbach" Marx says: "Thus, for instance, once the earthly family is discovered to be the secret of the holy family, the former must then itself be destroyed in theory and in practice". Engels, who made a number of editorial changes when he published the "Theses" in 1888, after Marx's death, altered the last part of this sentence to read: "must then itself be criticised in theory and transformed in practice". (Marx-Engels, *Collected Works,* Vol. 5, pp. 4, 7, 585). In *The German Ideology* (*Collected Works,* Vol. 5, pp. 75-6) Marx contrasts the family with what he calls "a communal domestic economy": "In all previous periods, however, the abolition [*Aufhebung*] of individual economy, which is inseparable from the abolition of private property, was impossible ... The setting up of a communal domestic economy presupposes the development of machinery, the use of natural forces and of many other productive forces ... the supersession of town and country. ... That the supersession of individual economy is inseparable from the supersession of the family is self-evident."

As regards "the supersession of town and country", according to Engels, writing in 1877-8, "abolition of the antithesis between town and country" has "become a direct necessity ... the great towns will perish". (*Anti-Dühring,* Part III, Chap. III, 1977, pp. 360-61).

Class divisions are dealt with in Marx's *Critique of the Gotha Programme.* The first phase of communism, says Marx, "recognises no class differences, because everyone is only a worker like everyone else". But as stated in *A Dictionary of Marxist Thought* (p.77) "class structure is a much more complex and ambiguous phenomenon than appears from most of the writings of Marx and Engels." And, as Nove says (p.19), "conflict is not only a matter of class war."

As for religion, it has been pointed out that in the unexpurgated German version of the *Critique of the Gotha Programme* (*Werke,* 19:31), in a reference to "bourgeois 'freedom of conscience'," Marx likens religious needs to excretory functions: "Everyone must be able to relieve his religious needs like his bodily needs, without the police sticking their noses in". Marx's opinion, as stated in interviews with a correspondent of the *Chicago Tribune* (published January 5, 1879), was that: "as socialism grows, religion will disappear." "We know", said Marx, "that violent measures against religion are nonsense; ... Its disappearance must be done by social development, in which education must play a great part." But when he was asked: "to carry out the principles of Socialism do its believers advocate assassination and bloodshed?," Marx answered: "No great movement has ever been inaugurated without bloodshed". (*Karl Marx Remembered*, ed. Philip S. Foner, 1983, pp. 259-60). This question and Marx's reply are not mentioned on pages 180, 318, 332 of Volume II of Richard N. Hunt's book, *The Political Ideas of Marx and Engels* (1984), where the *Chicago Tribune* article is quoted from and commented on, although on page 182 (see also page 179) Professor Hunt seeks to use Marx's and Engels's comments on religion to link them to "liberal democracy" and "Victorian decency".

To support these conclusions, Hunt evokes a peculiar malady which he attributes to Marx and Engels. "This malady," he says, was a "peculiar moral constipation", a "disorder from which both men suffered virtually all their lives". It was this "chronic difficulty in expressing a positive moral conviction", this "peculiar moral constipation that inhibited any straightforward defense of religious liberty on grounds of principle". This "same moral constipation", says Hunt, "whatever its cause, may have prevented Marx and Engels from defending on principle those individual *political* rights which in their Victorian decency they may also have taken for granted".

The plain fact, however, is that, as explained by Engels in 1871 and 1874, Marx and Engels calculated that "prohibiting religion in general" would be counter-productive and that if "atheism and materialism- which Bakunin himself learnt from us Germans- should be made obligatory" it would "drive away a vast number" of working men.

In the *Communist Manifesto* of 1848 Marx and Engels declared that "Communism abolishes eternal truths, it abolishes [*schafft ab*] all religion and all morality, ..." (*Collected Works,* Vol. 6, p. 504). But in July 1871 in a letter to Carlo Cafiero commenting on a Bakuninist proposal to make atheism and materialism obligatory for members of the International Working Men's Association, Engels wrote: "Marx and I are just as good old atheists and materialists as Bakunin, as indeed are most of our members, ... But to include all these things in our programme would mean to drive away a vast number of members, and to divide instead of uniting the European proletariat". (*Anarchism and Anarcho-Syndicalism*, Moscow, 1974, p. 50). And in an article written in June 1874 (Marx-Engels, *Selected Works* in three volumes, Volume Two, Moscow, 1977, p. 384) Engels said: "This much is certain: the only service that can still be rendered to God today is to make atheism a compulsory dogma and to surpass Bismarck's anticlerical *Kulturkampf* laws by prohibiting religion in general."

As a number of scholars have pointed out we also have much testimony to the effect that Marx had a "dictatorial" character. The Russian liberal P.V. Annenkov, for example, who visited Marx "by special invitation", observed of him that "He always spoke in imperative words that would brook no contradiction ..." and his "tone expressed the firm conviction of his mission to dominate men's minds and prescribe them their laws. Before me stood the embodiment of a democratic dictator such as one might imagine in a day dream". (Bruce Mazlish, *The Meaning of Karl Marx*, 1984, p. 69).

In his classic biography of Marx, Franz Mehring, "a founder of the Communist Party of Germany", quotes Carl Schurz's description of Marx: "... never in my life have I met a man whose attitude was so hurtfully and intolerably arrogant". (*Karl Marx: The Story of his Life*, 1981, p. 172). In his pen portrait of Marx, Schurz - who, says Nathaniel Weyl, was "a supporter of Lincoln" and a "crusader against Negro slavery" - testifies that: "... I was all the more eager to gather words of wisdom from the lips of that famous man. This expectation was disappointed in a peculiar way. ... To no opinion, which differed from his, he accorded the honor of even a condescending consideration. Everyone who contradicted him he treated with abject contempt; every argument that he did not like he answered either with biting scorn at the unfathomable ignorance that had prompted it, or with opprobious aspersions upon the motives of him who had advanced it." (N. Weyl, *Karl Marx: Racist*, 1979, pp. 206, 219-20). All this part of the description of Marx-which is taken from the *Autobiography of Carl Schurz* - has been excised from the quotation given in *Karl Marx: A Biography,* Second revised edition, Moscow, 1977, Third printing 1984, p. 181.

In September 1871 in a "Speech On The Seventh Anniversary Of The International" Marx declared that the working classes would have to conquer the right to emancipate themselves on the battlefield: "... But before such a change could be effected a proletarian *dictature* [dictatorship] would become necessary, and the first condition of that was a proletarian army. The working classes would have to conquer the right to emancipate themselves on the battlefield. The task of the International was to organize and combine the forces of labour for the coming struggle". (Karl Marx: *The First International and After,* Edited and Introduced by David Fernbach, Penguin Books, 1981, p. 272).

"Even for England and the United States", says Stanley Moore, "Marx did not rule out the possibility of civil war. He and his party, he wrote to Hyndman in 1880, considered an English revolution 'not *necessary,* but - according to historic precedents - *possible*'." And, in the next sentence, Marx added: "If the unavoidable evolution turns into a revolution, it would not only be the fault of the ruling classes, but also of the working class." If, Wolfe writes, in the last period of their lives, "Marx and Engels began to appreciate democracy as an instrument which their movement could use for its purposes, it was those purposes, and not democracy as such, on which their attention was concentrated". There are, says David Fernbach, "no general statements whatever" in Marx's work "affirming the normal possibility of a 'peaceful road' " to socialism. And, says Michael Evans, "the views of Marx and Engels were essentially the same". (Stanley Moore, *Three Tactics: The Background in Marx,* Monthly Review Press, 1963, p. 85; Bertram D. Wolfe, *Marxism,* p. 226, pp. 207-10; David Fernbach, *The First International and After,* 1981, p. 56; Michael Evans, *Karl Marx,* 1975, footnote 160 (Part III), pp. 193-4).

With regard to the national and racial divisions of mankind to which Bertell Ollman refers on pages 22, 34-36 and 38 of his article, *The Marxian Legacy,* first published by me in 1983 and now reprinted as Appendix I to the present volume, provides a concise collection of writings of Marx and Engels on Race, Nationalities, Colonialism and War, 1844-1894, and of what they said about the Slavs, Irish, Jews,

Blacks and others. Ollman is oblivious to "Marx's and Engels's fundamentally Eurocentric approach to social change". (Ian Cummins, *Marx, Engels and National Movements,* 1980, pp. 5, 175). "Marx and Engels, as Nimni suggests, were far from immune to" the "rabidly ethnocentric style of analysis and expression" of the 19th century "belief in the over-arching superiority of white Europe - often coupled with a belief in the exceptional racial and cultural superiority of some national group within it". (*Marxist Sociology Revisited,* Edited by Martin Shaw, 1985, Chapter 5, p. 146, and Chapter 4).

Ollman acknowledges on page 38 of his article that "It should be clear by now that Marx is far more precise about the social and other divisions which will disappear in communism than about what will replace them". Examples of the functional units into which communist society is divided are, says Ollman, "the factory, the communal domestic economy, and the industrial army for agriculture".

Ollman's conclusion (pp. 39-40), on the basis of his reconstruction of Marx's concept of communism and "the unproven assumptions on which this expected flowering of human nature rests", is that: "the citizen of the future", in communism, is someone who is "skilful in carrying out a variety of tasks, who is highly and consistently cooperative, who conceives of all objects in terms of 'ours', who shares with his fellow men a masterful control over the forces of nature, who regulates his activities without the help of externally imposed rules, and who is indistinguishable from his fellows when viewed from the perspective of existing social divisions. He (she) is, in short, a brilliant, highly rational and socialized, humane and successful creator". This, and the rest of Ollman's article, only serves to confirm, however, that, as indicated on the cover of Alec Nove's *The Economics of Feasible Socialism* (1983), Marx's ideas on what a communist economy might be like were "romantic and Utopian, with virtually all economic and social problems assumed out of existence."

In *Rubel on Karl Marx* (1981), five essays by Maximilien Rubel "based on many years of pioneering textual research" are presented in English translation for the first time. On page 229, Rubel states that Marx added to the rigorous methodological plan for the "Economics" as the scientific critique of capital and the state, another project no less methodical in its form and portentous in its significance: "to reveal the 'rational core' of utopia as the model of a human environment that is to be constructed by a species now at the crossroads of its destiny".

Seventy years before the publication in English of Rubel's collection of essays, O.D. Skelton, in a prize winning book, pointed out that "the cleavage between Utopian and scientific or Marxian socialism is probably not so deep as has been contended by some exponents of Marxism ...; much that has usually been ascribed to Marx is found in germ, at least, among his predecessors." The founders of the Marxian faith "looked forward with a trustful optimism inherited from their Utopian forerunners to the time when voluntary organizations cooperating harmoniously would serve all men's needs". (*Socialism: A Critical Analysis,* 1911, pp. 62, 185).

Maurice Meisner, in *Marxism, Maoism and Utopianism* (1982, pp. 7-8, 13), asks how it was that Marx projected a vision of the future communist utopia yet condemned as "utopian" (and thus reactionary) similar socialist and communist visions. "It was not the ends the utopian socialists sought that made them 'utopian' in the Marxist sense", says Meisner, "but rather the inadequacy of the means proposed to achieve those ends. ... On the one hand, Marxism projects a utopian vision of a communist future that is seen as immanent in the history of the present. On the other hand, Marxist theory condemns as 'utopian' socialist ideas and visions which it associates with the early stages of capitalism, which it identifies as crude ideological reflections of the backward conditions of pre-industrial society, ..."

According to E.H. Carr (*The Bolshevik Revolution* 1917-1923, Vol. 1, (1950) 1984, p. 255), "the dichotomy in Marxist thought [which] combined a highly realist and relativist analysis of the historical process with an uncompromisingly absolute vision of the ultimate goal, and strove to bridge the gap between them by a chain of causal development. This transformation of reality into utopia, of the relative into the absolute, of incessant class conflict into the classless society, and of the ruthless use of state power into the stateless society, was the essence of what Marx and Lenin believed. In so far as this was inconsistent, the inconsistency was fundamental."

There are, suggests Professor Nove, "harmless and harmful utopias." It is, he feels, important for Marxists to face up to the objection that the 'ideal society' of Marx's romantic imagination is "unreal" and "that what is proposed is an unrealisable utopia". Nove's important work is not an anti-socialist treatise and what it demonstrates is that Marx's ideas on communism are "very seriously defective and misleading". And this kind of utopian thinking, Nove contends, "must actively mislead, must direct along irrelevant or dangerous roads, anyone who takes it seriously". (op.cit., pp. x, 13, 15, 239, and *passim*). Domenico Settembrini comes to much the same conclusions in Part Two of *Marxian Utopia?* (Centre for Research into Communist Economies, 1985).

For a further discussion of some aspects of this subject see "Marxism And Dirty Hands", a recent essay by Steven Lukes in *Marxism And Liberalism,* edited by Paul, Miller, Paul and Ahrens (Blackwell, 1986). Other essays in this volume include "The Marxist Conceptual Framework And The Origins Of Totalitarian Socialism" by Allen E. Buchanan, "Marxian Freedom, Individual Liberty, And The End Of Alienation" by John Gray, and "Marxism, Violence, And Tyranny" by George Friedman.

The Illegitimate Son

There are, of course, aspects of Marx's life and thought which have come to light since Schwarzschild's book was written, and subsequent writers have elaborated themes which Schwarzschild introduced. The matter of the illegitimate son, Henry Frederick Demuth, is dealt with by Werner Blumenberg (1962), Yvonne Kapp (1972 and 1983), Fritz J. Raddatz (1975), in Robert Payne's *Marx* (1968), and elsewhere. (66) "There can be no reasonable doubt," says Kapp, "that he [Frederick Demuth] was Marx's son", in which case, writes Raddatz: Marx "lived an almost lifelong lie, scorned, humiliated, and disowned his only surviving son. The spectacle of the Sunday order of march over Hampstead Heath with Hélène Demuth [Frederick's mother and Marx's servant] trailing behind carrying the provisions basket is not merely humiliating but disgraceful." (67)

In her will, Hélène Demuth, after a lifetime of service to Marx and Engels, left everything she had (£95) to her son who was referred to as "Frederick Lewis Demuth". Raddatz says that Lewis was the name of Frederick's foster parents and, according to Padover (1980), a death certificate naming "Frederick Lewis Demuth" is "displayed in the Karl-Marx-Haus" in Trier, Marx's birthplace in Germany. (68) A newly discovered photograph of Freddy Demuth: "Marx's secret son" was published in "The Times" on August 18, 1972.

In a typed copy of a three page letter reported by Blumenberg to have been written to August Bebel (September 2/4, 1898), Louise Freyberger, Engels's former secretary and housekeeper, says: "...That Freddy Demuth is Marx's son, I know from General [Engels] himself. ... Freddy looks ridiculously like Marx and, with that typically Jewish face and blue-black hair, it was really only blind prejudice that could see in him any resemblance to General...". "There is no doubt", says McLellan, "of the general credibility of this letter". (69) "Engels's part was to assume, until he lay on his death-bed, the fictitious paternity of Freddy Demuth" (Kapp, 1983), to cover up for Marx and to avoid the scandal which could have destroyed Marx politically.

In a contribution to *Marx: 100 Years On* (edited by the Marxist Betty Matthews, 1983, pp. 216-17), Michèle Barrett, supposing that Kapp is right, says that "the Demuth issue does identify the secrecy and hypocrisy that formed part of Marx family life". And she refers to "the painful fact that, as far as feminism is concerned, Marx's feet really are made of clay". As McLellan points out, "the price of Marx's vocation was high: of his seven [legitimate] children (one died at birth) only two survived him, and both of them committed suicide."

Marx's Finances

On page 144 of his book (1948 edition) Schwarzschild says that many of Marx's acquaintances thought that he was living on too grand a scale and that his wife Jenny, the daughter of a noble family, did not know much about housekeeping; also that Marx neither had nor sought any kind of steady income. Marx's financial circumstances are also examined in some detail, for example, by Raddatz and by David McLellan in *Karl Marx : Interviews and Recollections* (1981) and *Karl Marx : The Legacy* (1983). "In fact," says McLellan, "the Marx family were never poor by ordinary standards: their income even in the worst years was about three times that earned by an average skilled workman. Marx's difficulties were caused by his pride, his desire to keep up appearances and his almost total inability to manage his financial resources. ... In his worst years Marx's income was never less than £200 a year. In the early 1850's £150 was considered quite an adequate income for a lower-middle-class family with three children. Skilled workers earned about £50 a year, a bank clerk about £75 a year. ... The family had always had one servant (and for a few years there was a second one). The children were sent to private schools and had extra lessons in music and drama." (McLellan 1983, p.39; 1981 p.xvii).

Marx's speculations on the stock exchange are mentioned in a letter he wrote (June 25, 1864) to his uncle Lion Philips, founder of the business concern whch, Payne says, was eventually to become the giant Philips Electrical Company. By speculating "partly in American funds, but particularly in English stocks", said Marx, "I won more than £400 and will now, when the entanglement of political conditions offers new scope, begin anew." (S.K. Padover, *The Letters of Karl Marx*, 1979, p. 187; Marx-Engels *Werke*, Vol. 30, 1964, p.665).

Some Other Aspects

Some revealing early works of Karl Marx such as his essay "The Union Of Believers With Christ According To John 15:1-14, Showing Its Basis And Essence, Its Absolute Necessity, And Its Effects", and his poetic drama *Oulanem*, are discussed in Robert Payne's *Marx* (1968) and *The Unknown Karl Marx* (1972). Payne and Arnold Künzli (author of the massive *Karl Marx: Eine Psychographie*, 1966) are simply excluded from consideration and dismissed with an abusive epithet ("the gutter school of marxology") by the Marxist writer Hal Draper (*Karl Marx's Theory Of Revolution*, Vol. 1, 1977, p.704). A temperate survey of works by Künzli, Payne and others may be found in Herbert Moller's review essay in *History And Theory*, Vol.VIII, No. 3, 1969.

On page 194 (see also pp. 151, 185) of *The Red Prussian (1948)* Schwarzschild quotes references by Marx and Engels to the peasants as "the barbarians of civilization". On the peasant question there is also David Mitrany's *Marx Against the Peasant: A Study in Social Dogmatism* (1961) and Esther Kingston-Mann's *Lenin And The Problem Of Marxist Peasant Revolution* (1983). Chapter 1 of the latter work is called "The Lessons of the Marxist Classics".

Lewis S. Feuer, Margaret A. Fay, and Ralph Colp Jr. have exploded the Marx-Darwin myth. See also my *Marx and Darwin* (1983) reprinted as Appendix II to the present volume.

Examples of Marx's anti-Jewish and anti-semitic writings are dealt with in Chapters 5, 12 and 13 of Schwarzschild's book, and as one reviewer said when the book was first published, Mr. Schwarzschild "convicts Marx by quoting him". This subject has since been investigated in great detail by Julius Carlebach in his *Karl Marx and the Radical Critique of Judaism* (1978); by Robert Wistrich in his *Revolutionary Jews From Marx to Trotsky* (1976) and *Socialism and the Jews* (1982); by Nathaniel Weyl *(Karl Marx : Racist,* 1979), Diane Paul (1981) who refers to Hal Draper's "greatly exaggerated" argument of 1977, Joseph Clark (1981), Michael Billig (1984), and others. (70)

NOTES

1.   David Felix, *Marx As Politician* (1983), pp. 285-87.

2.   *Political Studies,* Vol. XXIX No. 1 (1981), p.117. See also Kolakowski's reply, pp. 123-25.

3.   *New Society,* November 3, 1983.

4.   Marx-Engels, *Collected Works,* Vol. 3 (London, 1975), p.406.

5.   Allen Oakley, *Marx's Critique of Political Economy,* Vol. 1 (1984), p. 10. "Nor is there any evidence", says Michael Evans, "of acquaintance with political economy in Marx's articles for the *Rheinische Zeitung*" (on the debates on the law on thefts of wood, the economic conditions of the Moselle peasantry, etc.). Marx became one of the editors of the *Rheinische Zeitung* in October 1842 but resigned in March 1843. (Michael Evans, "Karl Marx's first confrontation with political economy: the 1844 Manuscripts", in *Economy and Society,* Vol. 13, No. 2, May 1984, pp. 115-16).

In the *Economic-Philosophical Manuscripts of 1844,* says Wolfe *(Marxism,* pp. 362-63), the young Marx had just begun his reductivism - the reduction of "the essential problems of the human condition, and of the philosophy he had learned, to problems in economics".

6.   *Studies On The Left,* Vol. 7 No. 1 (1967), pp. 24-25.

7.   Angus Walker, *Marx: His Theory And Its Context* (1978), p. 19.

8.   Henri Arvon, *La Philosophie Allemande* (1970), p.90.

9.   Felix, op. cit., p.131. "It was not primarily through the study of economics", says Robert Tucker, "that Marx was led to his economic interpretation of history; he came to it by the philosophical path. ... Marx created his own system on the basis of a misreading of Hegel". (*Philosophy And Myth In Karl Marx,* 1967, pp. 26, 123). See also Franz Wiedmann, *Hegel,* New York, 1968, Chapter 8, "The Hegelian Schools", and Chapter 9, "Hegel and Marxism".

10. Frederick Engels, *The Peasant War in Germany,* Third authorised edition, 1875, Addendum to Preface (1977), p. 22.

The nature of the intellectual relationship between Marx and Engels, which lasted for more than 38 years up to Marx's death in 1883, is still being hotly debated - see for example, the article by Stanley and Zimmermann "On the Alleged Differences Between Marx and Engels" and the rejoinder by Terrell Carver in *Political Studies* (1984) XXXII, pp. 226-256. As Neven Sesardić says in *Marxian Utopia?* (Sesardić and Settembrini, 1985, p.40) some commentators on Marx and Marxism "pretend to understand Marx better than he understood himself".

What is not denied is that in 1860 in *Herr Vogt* Marx wrote: "I mention Engels because we work to a common plan and after prior agreement." (Marx-Engels, *Collected Works,* Vol.17, p.114). This, says Terrell Carver, refers to the *political journalism* of Marx and Engels. But again, in 1865, as indicated by Schwarzschild (p.103) Marx - who was then "working like a horse" on *Das Kapital* - said of himself and Engels: "we two are running a joint partnership, to which I contribute my time for theoretical and party business." (Letter to Engels dated 31 July, 1865, in Saul K. Padover, *The Letters of Karl Marx,* 1979, p.198; Marx-Engels, *Werke,* Vol.31, 1965, p.131).

And fifteen years later, in 1880, Marx wrote a Foreword to the French edition of Engels's pamphlet *Socialism: Utopian and Scientific,* which was an extract (of three chapters) from Engels's book *Anti-Dühring* (1878) with a few extra remarks added by Engels. The last sentence of the Foreword stated that "In this pamphlet we present the extract which best characterizes the theoretical part of the book [i.e. *Anti-Dühring*], and which constitutes what may be called an *introduction to scientific socialism.*" (see F. Engels, *Socialism: Utopian and Scientific,* Peking, 1975, pp.1-4 and Notes).

Marx also wrote one of the chapters of *Anti-Dühring,* on the history of economic theories, and, says Schwarzschild (p.368), this "work of both Marx and Engels ... was to figure later as the second most important document of Marxian socialism."

11. Marx-Engels, *Selected Correspondence* (London, 1941), p.102.

12. Marx, *Capital,* Vol. 1 Part III Chap. XI (1983), p.292.

13. Engels, *Anti-Dühring,* Moscow, 1977, Part 1 Chap. XII, p.155.

14. Marx-Engels, *Selected Correspondence* (London, 1941), pp. 494-495.

15. Lenin, *Collected Works,* Vol. 38 (1972), p.180.

16. Engels, "Marx and the *Neue Rheinische Zeitung*" (1884) in Marx-Engels, *Selected Works,* Moscow, 1958, Vol. II, p.300.

17. Marx-Engels, *Collected Works,* Vol. 7, p.437.

18. Marx-Engels, *Collected Works,* Vol. 5, p.209.

19. Saul K. Padover, *The Essential Marx: The Non-Economic Writings* (1979), Chap. VIII, Press And Censorship, p.280. See also p.262: "For Marx was now not the liberal newspaper-

man of 1842-43, but an embattled communist. His interest was no longer in freedom of the press but in the overthrow of the whole 'bourgeois' social order."

20.   Marx-Engels, *Collected Works*, Vol. 7, p.506.

21.   Marx-Engels, *Selected Works* (Moscow, 1977), Vol. 2, p.379.

22.   *Capital*, Vol. 1 Part VIII Chap. XXXI (1983), p.703.

23.   Marx-Engels, *Collected Works*, Vol. 6, p.503.

24.   See my collection of writings of Marx and Engels on Race, Nationalities, Colonialism and War, 1844-1894: *The Marxian Legacy* (first published 1983), Third edition, 1987, at Appendix I to the present volume, pp. 102-03, 112.

25.   Ian Cummins, *Marx, Engels and National Movements* (1980), pp. 34, 38, 40. A letter by Marx, written some 13 years later, in which "all his prejudices and all the fury of vulgar racism seem to have combined" is cited on page 246 of Léon Poliakov's *The Aryan Myth: A History Of Racist And Nationalist Ideas In Europe* (1977).

26.   David McLellan, *Karl Marx: His Life and Thought* (1973), p.214.

27.   Marx-Engels, *Collected Works*, Vol. 38 (1982), p.182.

28.   For the complete text see Marx-Engels, *Collected Works*, Vol. 4, p.36.

29.   Marx-Engels, *Collected Works*, Vol. 4, p.37.

30.   *Capital*, Vol. 1 Part 4 Chap. XV Section 1 (1983), p.352.

31.   *Selected Correspondence* (1941), p.7; Marx-Engels, *Collected Works*, Vol. 38, 1982, p.96.

32.   Marx-Engels, *Collected Works*, Vol. 6, p.166.

33. See my review in *The Freethinker,* Vol. 92, No. 51, 16 December, 1972.

34. On page 28 of *Karl Marx: The Legacy* (1983), McLellan writes: "The transition to communism was inevitable: 'Communism is not for us a state of affairs still to be established, not an ideal to which reality will have to adjust. We call communism the real movement which abolishes the present state of affairs.' (*German Ideology*)."

35. *New Left Review,* Jan. - Feb. 1981.

36. Marx-Engels, *Selected Correspondence* (1941), pp.475-76, 484, 510, 516-18. Karl Federn, *The Materialist Conception of History* (1939), p.223.

37. M.M. Bober, *Karl Marx's Interpretation of History* (1965), p.310.

38. Vladimir G. Simkhovitch, *Marxism Versus Socialism* (London, n.d., ? 1913) p. 33.

39. Graeme Duncan, *Marx And Mill* (1973), pp. 142-43.

40. Alec Nove, *The Economics of Feasible Socialism* (1983), pp.62-64.

41. Marx, *Capital,* Vol. 1 (1983), Part 1 Chap. 1 Section 1, p.46, Section 4, pp.76, 78; Vol. III (1977), Part 1 Chap. II, p.43, Part II Chap. IX, p.168. For a further critique of the philosophy of "essence" in *Capital,* see e.g., Kolakowski, op.cit.(1978), Vol. 1, Chap. XIII; K.R. Popper, *The Open Society And Its Enemies,* Vol. II, p.177.

42. Michio Morishima and George C. Catephores, *Value, Exploitation and Growth* (1978), p.189.

43. Jerrold Seigel, *Marx's Fate* (1978), p.323; Marx, *Economic And Philosophic Manuscripts of 1844* (1959), p.30.

44. Terrell Carver, "Marx's Commodity Fetishism", *Inquiry,* 18

(1975), p.39. Marx's argument at the beginning of *Capital*, by elimination of everything except human labour, is, says Carver (p.45), "very much the work of an old-fashioned natural philosopher". And Marx himself, a few pages later, says that the labour must be useful and "socially necessary".

45. Cornelius Castoriadis, *Crossroads in the Labyrinth* (1984), Chapter on "Value, Equality, Justice, Politics: From Marx to Aristotle and from Aristotle to Ourselves", p.263.

46. H.W.B. Joseph, *The Labour Theory of Value in Karl Marx* (1923), pp. 26, 42, 62, 64, 90-92, 100.

47. Morishima and Catephores, op.cit., p.185.

48. Joan Robinson, *Further Contributions to Modern Economics* (1980), p.199.

49. Seigel, op.cit., p.361. Cf. pp. 303 ff. on Marx's *Grundrisse*.

50. Nove, op.cit., p.26. For a critical analysis of Marx's notion of labour "embodied or materialised" in commodities, see Terrell Carver, op.cit., 1975, pp.54-60.

51. Ernest Mandel and Alan Freeman (Editors), *Ricardo, Marx, Sraffa* (1984), pp. xiv, xv.

52. Jon Elster, on page 118 of his recently published work (see p. 28 of the present volume), states that Marx's analysis of capitalism as an economic system "rests on two main pillars: the labour theory of value and the theory of the falling rate of profit. Both have conclusively been shown to be invalid". Professor Elster's book argues that Marx's economic theories are largely wrong or irrelevant, and historical materialism is seen to have only limited plausibility (and is not even consistently applied by Marx). The book claims to provide a systematic criticism of functionalism and teleological thinking in Marx.

53. *Selected Correspondence* (1941), p.39; Marx-Engels, *Werke*, Vol. 27 (1963), p.278.

54. Marx-Engels, *Collected Works*, Vol. 10, pp. 277-287.

A book by Richard N. Hunt, *The Political Ideas of Marx and Engels* (Vol. 1, 1975), tries to explain away what Marx and Engels actually stated in the *Communist Manifesto,* the *New Rhenish Gazette,* the March 1850 *Address,* and elsewhere. Hunt suggests that the *March Address* and the *Communist Manifesto* do not express Marx and Engels' real views (pp.236, 248); that the *Address* was "the work of a committee" which was internally divided (pp.242,243); that it was drawn up on behalf of the committee by Marx and Engels who "were obliged to eat humble pie" (pp.235, 240, 243); and that, in parallel with the *Manifesto,* it "involved compromise formulations on the key issues" (pp. 257, 246, 191). Hunt also claims that in the concluding paragraphs of the *Manifesto* "Marx and Engels did not really mean what they appear to say" (p.177); that their "later recollections [in regard to the drawing up of the *Manifesto*] are surely exaggerated" (p.188); and so on.

Professor Hunt maintains these views whilst admitting (p.242) that: "Unfortunately, we know even less about how the *Circular* [or *Address*] was drawn up than in the case of the Manifesto. Stylistic analysis would seem to confirm Marx's and Engels' authorship, as would Marx's twice-repeated reference to the document 'composed [verfasste] by Engels and myself' ". In fact, in a letter to Engels dated 13 July, 1851, Marx refers to "the address to the League which we drew up together". And Hunt fails in this section of his book dealing with the *March Address* to quote or mention Marx's explicit declaration, in the same letter, that the March Address to the Communist League was "at bottom nothing but a plan of war [Kriegsplan] against democracy [die Democratie]".

Hunt is likewise of the opinion that: "the *New Rhenish Gazette* utterances must indeed be understood as outbursts of rage" (p.248); that "the terror passages ... really were impotent cries of rage" and "even as visions of revenge they seem fairly pale" (p.203); that the "revolting genocidal outburst" in the *New Rhenish Gazette* "was clearly a temporary aberration" (p.201); and so forth.

Hunt's views are criticised by Seigel (1978) and rejected by Steven Seidman (*Liberalism and the Origins of European Social Theory,* 1983, pp.114, 118-19). For Hunt, the pronouncements in the *New Rhenish Gazette* are "clearly a temporary aberration, born in the anguished helplessness of defeat". But, says Seidman, we find similar 'aberrations' in the writings of Marx and Engels (*The Poverty of Philosophy,* the *Communist Manifesto*) prior to the defeats of 1848. "Marx's language [in the *Manifesto*] - 'Communists support every revolutionary movement' - covers and legitimates any and all forms of self-proclaimed revolutionary movements. Marx failed to discriminate between legitimate and illegitimate forms and means of revolution; ... Marx's ambiguity was not simply one of language and wording but one of concept." "It simply will not do", Seidman says, "to assimilate Marx to the contemporary disposition of social democrats".

Seigel also warns (op.cit., pp.420, 423) that "Hunt's general thesis that Marx and Engels were democrats must be taken with some reserve" and he argues against Hunt's attempt to attribute the sentiments of the *March Address* to other members of the Communist League rather than to Marx and Engels.

Ideas exactly similar to Hunt's are refuted in detail in Special Note E (pp. 599-612) in Volume II of Hal Draper's *Karl Marx's Theory Of Revolution,* 1978. "The *Address*", Draper concludes, is "an expression of the views of Marx and Engels, which *mutatis mutandum* continued to reflect their political thought right up to the end.".

55.   Quoted by Schwarzschild, op.cit., 1948, p.272.

56.   *Selected Correspondence* (1941), p. 227.

57.   Marx, *Letters to Dr. Kugelmann* (London, 1941), pp. 102, 106, 107.

58.   Felix, op. cit., pp. 161-62, 269-70. *Karl Marx : The First International and After,* Penguin Books (1974, Reprinted 1981), pp. 73-81. A comparison of Marx's sentence with the

reports of both "The Morning Star" and "The Times" makes it absolutely clear that it is a piecing together of selected parts of sentences which appear in the reports, with words preceding and intervening, omitted. This nullifies the sense of what Gladstone said in his budget speech of 1863, as both Tsuzuki and Felix point out, and as Felix shows in more detail, it is a falsification.

59.   Fritz J. Raddatz, *Karl Marx: A Political Biography,* English edn. 1979, p.147 - see also p.257 (Orig. 1975). In his valuable article of May 1984 (see Note 5) Michael Evans observes that Marx "in some respects grossly distorts [Adam] Smith's meaning". (p.146; see also pp. 126, 143, 144).

60.   *Karl Marx : A Biography,* Moscow, 1973, p.428.

61.   *Bebel's Reminiscences,* Part 1, New York (1911), p.207.

62.   *Capital,* Vol. III, Chap. XXIII (1984), p.383.

63.   Saul K. Padover, *Karl Marx: On Education, Women, and Children* (1975), pp.91, 131.

64.   Nove, op.cit., pp. 50-54.

65.   *The First International and After* (see Note 58), p.324. As Graeme Duncan remarks (*Marx And Mill,* p.160), Marx's Amsterdam speech is commonly quoted as if it referred only to the two or three countries where the workers might attain their goal by peaceful means. Marx's next sentence stating that "in most continental countries the lever of the revolution will have to be force" etc. is, says Duncan, "quoted less commonly". This sentence is not included, for example, in the quotation given on page 446 of Professor Jon Elster's *Making Sense of Marx* (1985).

66.   Werner Blumenberg, *Karl Marx,* English edition, 1972. Yvonne Kapp, *Eleanor Marx,* Vol. 1 (1972; reprinted 1979); "Karl Marx's Children : Family Life 1844-1855" in *Marx : 100 Years On* (1983), pp.273-305. H.F. Peters, *Red Jenny: A*

Life With Karl Marx, 1986, pp. 104-5.

67.   Kapp (1979), p.279; Raddatz (1979), p.134.

68.   Raddatz (1979), p.134; Saul K. Padover, *Karl Marx: An Intimate Biography,* Abridged Edition (1980), p.294.

69.   Blumenberg (1972), pp. 123-24; Raddatz (1979), pp.135-36, 293; Padover (1980), pp. 304-5; McLellan (1973), pp. 271-72.

70.   Diane Paul, *Journal of the History of Ideas,* Jan. - March 1981; Joseph Clark, *Dissent,* Winter 1981; Michael Billig, *Patterns of Prejudice,* January and April 1984. See also, e.g., Edna Healey, *Wives of Fame: Mary Livingstone, Jenny Marx, Emma Darwin* (1986), pp.74, 109, and my collection, *The Marxian Legacy* (1983), Third edition, 1987, at Appendix I to the present volume.

APPENDIX I

The Marxian Legacy

Race, Nationalities, Colonialism and War

Compiled by Leslie R. Page

KARL MARX AND FRIEDRICH ENGELS

WRITINGS NOT GENERALLY KNOWN

on

RACE, NATIONALITIES, COLONIALISM AND WAR

1844-1894

WHAT MARX AND ENGELS SAID ABOUT

THE SLAVS, IRISH, JEWS, BLACKS AND OTHERS

ISBN 0 907671 07 1

Third edition (with some additions) 1987

FOREWORD

Karl Marx died in 1883. As his contribution to the centenary celebrations Leslie Page has in this short pamphlet collected a few choice yet altogether typical Marxist judgements on race, nationalities, colonialism and war. These are all judgements made either by Marx, or by his lifelong collaborator Friedrich Engels, or by both together. Nevertheless, perhaps not very surprisingly, Leslie Page again and again finds himself noting that some especially rich saying has been omitted from the most recent and the most widely circulated editions.

First reactions to the present pamphlet are likely to differ a lot according to the generation of the reader. Almost everyone, surely, will be shocked by the coarse racism, the brutal exultation in "the most determined use of terror" and the contemptuous advocacy of the assimilation or extermination of inferior, "petty, hidebound nations". But those of us who lived through the 1930's and early 1940's will be irresistibly reminded of Adolf Hitler and his National Socialists (Nazis), of Benito Mussolini and his Facists, and will wonder how either of these movements could have come to be seen as diametrically opposed to Marxism-Leninism. The younger generations - deafened throughout their whole lives by the drumfire of Marxist-Leninist denunciations of racism, colonialism and imperialism - will be astonished to discover that the Founding Fathers of international socialism said innumerable things which, certainly if said by anyone perceived as "right-wing", would today be universally accepted as racist, colonialist and imperialist.

All this should suggest just how ruinously wrong it is to think of Marxist-Leninists and of National Socialists or Fascists as being at opposite ends of the political spectrum: the former on the extreme left wing; and the latter on the extreme right wing. (Adolf Hitler himself made no such mistake. For he knew how many recruits came to him straight from the Communist Party, and privately insisted that they were to be welcomed as natural Nazi material. Sometime "bourgeois liberals", conservatives or social-democrats must, however, by the same token, always remain suspect.) The truth is that both sorts of movement - Marxist-Leninist and Nazi - are through and through what Sir Karl Popper calls "historicist", believing in historical inevitabilities in which the only right is might. Both sorts are committed to the all-powerful, all-intrusive totalitarian state - states under the absolute and irremovable power of the controlling élite of the monopoly party.

Which is where The Freedom Association comes in. For we, as our name proclaims, stand for the maximum of individual freedom under the rule of equal and non-discriminatory laws, for liberal and elective democracy and for a minimal state. The Freedom Association is promoting the present pamphlet in order to show how much the Marxist-Leninists and the National Socialists have in common, and precisely where in the writings of the Founding Fathers Mr Andropov and his associates could find authoritative Marxist warrant for many of their most obnoxious policies.

You ask about red terror in Cambodia, or Ethiopia, or wherever else? Remember the endorsement given by Engels to "the most determined use of terror". About Soviet anti-semitism and the stubborn refusal to "Let my people go"? Reread the rantings of Marx against all (other) Jews, and against everything Jewish. What, then, about Soviet colonialism in Eastern Europe, and the cruel and murderous expansion of the Soviet Empire into Afghanistan? Well, here is Engels again, on the Prussian seizure of part of Denmark: "It is the right of civilization as against barbarism, of progress as against stability ... the right of historical evolution."

Antony Flew: A founder-member of the Council of the Freedom Association, formerly Professor of Philosophy in the University of Reading   *May 1983*

Further Reading

Robert Wesson,   *Why Marxism?* (London: Temple Smith 1976).

Nathaniel Weyl,   *Karl Marx: Racist* (New Rochelle, N.Y.: Arlington House, 1979).

Shlomo Avineri,   *Karl Marx on Colonialism and Modernization* (New York: Doubleday Anchor, 1969).

R.N. Carew-Hunt,   *The Theory and Practice of Communism* (Harmondsworth: Penguin, 1963).

K.R. Popper,   *The Open Society and its Enemies* (Routledge and Kegan Paul, 5th edition, 1966), Vol. II.

GENERAL

"... the productiveness of labour is fettered by physical conditions. These are all referable to the constitution of man himself (race etc.) and to surrounding Nature." Marx, *Capital* (1867), Vol. 1 Part V Chap. XVI.

"The possibility is here presented for definite economic development taking place, depending of course, upon favourable circumstances, inborn racial characteristics, etc." Marx, *Capital,* Vol. 3 Chap. XLVII.

"By recognising the inheritance of acquired characteristics it [modern natural science] extends the subject of experience from the individual to the genus;... If, for instance, among us the mathematical axioms seem self-evident to every eight-year-old child, and in no need of proof from experience, this is solely the result of "accumulated inheritance". It would be difficult to teach them by a proof to a bushman or Australian negro." Engels, "Notes to Anti-Dühring" (1884-85), in *Anti-Dühring,* Moscow, 1977, pp. 443-44.

"The plentiful meat and milk diet among the Aryans and the Semites, and particularly the beneficial effects of these foods on the development of children, may, perhaps, explain the superior development of these two races." Engels, *Origin of the Family, Private Property and the State,* Fourth revised edition, 1891, in Marx-Engels, *Selected Works In One Volume,* Lawrence & Wishart: London, 1980, p.464. (Marx, in 1880-81, made notes on Lewis Morgan's book *Ancient Society* (1877), and Engels, when writing *Origin of the Family, Private Property and the State* in 1884, made a wide use of Marx's notes and his propositions and the material derived from Morgan's book).

"We regard economic conditions as that which ultimately determines historical development. But race is itself an economic factor." Engels to W. Borgius, January 25, 1894. Marx-Engels, *Selected Correspondence,* Third revised edition, Moscow, 1975, p.441. (A note in the 1968 edition of Marx-Engels, *Selected Works In One Volume,* states that W. Borgius was wrongly identified in all previous editions as H. Starkenburg. Borgius had put the following question to Engels: What part is played by the *racial* element and by historic *personality* in Marx and Engels' conception of history? See Marx-Engels, *Selected Correspondence,* Lawrence & Wishart: London, 1943. p.519).

"Even naturally evolved differences within the species, such as racial differences, etc., which Sancho [Stirner] does not mention at all, can and must be abolished in the course of historical development." Marx and Engels, *The German Ideology* (1845-46), *Collected Works,* Lawrence & Wishart: London, 1975-, Vol. 5 p.425.

THE EXTERMINATION OF ENTIRE PEOPLES

"Among all the large and small nations of Austria only three standard-bearers of progress took an active part in history, and still retain their vitality - the Germans, the Poles and the Magyars. Hence they are now revolutionary. All the other large and small nationalities and peoples are destined to perish before long in the revolutionary world storm. ... There is no country in Europe which does not have in some corner or other several ruined fragments of peoples, the remnant of a former population that was suppressed and held in bondage by the nation which later became the main vehicle of historical development. These relics of a nation mercilessly trampled under foot in the course of history, as Hegel says, these *residual fragments of peoples* always become fanatical standard-bearers of counter-revolution and remain so until their complete extirpation or loss of their national character, just as their whole existence in general is itself a protest against a great historical revolution...the Austrian Germans and Magyars will be set free and wreak a bloody revenge on the Slav barbarians. The general war which will then break out will smash this Slav Sonderbund [League] and wipe out all these petty, hidebound nations down to their very names. The next world war will result in the disappearance from the face of the earth not only of reactionary classes and dynasties, but also of entire reactionary peoples. And that, too, is a step forward." Engels, "The Magyar Struggle" (article in the *Neue Rheinische Zeitung* - hereafter referred to as NRZ - January 13, 1849), *Collected Works,* Vol. 8, pp.230, 234, 238. (Marx wielded absolute power over what went into the NRZ. In an article "Marx and the Neue Rheinische Zeitung" published in 1884 Engels stated: "The editorial constitution was simply the dictatorship of Marx." See Marx-Engels, *Selected Works,* Moscow, 1958, Vol. II p.300. This statement of Engels was ignored by Roman Rosdolsky in his essay "Friedrich Engels and the Problem of 'Historyless' Peoples", 1964 - see Julius Carlebach, *Karl Marx and the Radical Critique of Judaism,* 1978, p.423).

"...hatred of Russia was and still is the *primary revolutionary passion* among Germans; that since the revolution, hatred of Czechs and Croats has been added, and that only by the most determined use of terror against these Slav peoples can we, jointly with the Poles and Magyars, safeguard the revolution." Engels, "Democratic Pan-Slavism" (*NRZ* February 16, 1849), *Collected Works,* Vol. 8 p.378.

DYING NATIONALITIES: THEIR INEVITABLE SUBMISSION TO ABSORPTION INTO A MORE ENERGETIC STOCK

"Neither Bohemia nor Croatia was strong enough to exist as a nation by herself. Their respective nationalities, gradually undermined by the action of historical causes that inevitably absorbs them into a more energetic stock, could only hope to be restored to something like independence by an alliance with other Slavonic nations ... Scattered remnants of numerous nations, whose nationality and political vitality had long been extinguished, ... the same as the Welsh in England, the Basques in Spain, the Bas-Bretons in France, and at a more recent period the Spanish and French Creoles in those portions of North America occupied of late by the Anglo-American race - these dying nationalities, the Bohemians, Carinthians, Dalmations, etc., had tried...to restore their political *status quo* of A.D. 800. The history of a thousand years ought to have shown them that such a retrogression was impossible; ... this fact merely proved the historical tendency, and at the same time the physical and intellectual power of the German nation to subdue, absorb, and assimilate its ancient eastern neighbours; that this tendency of absorption on the part of the Germans had always been and still was one of the mightiest means by which the civilization of western Europe had been spread in the east of that Continent; ... and that, therefore, the natural and inevitable fate of these dying nations was to allow this progress of dissolution and absorption by their stronger neighbours to complete itself." Signed by Marx but written by Engels, *Revolution and Counter-Revolution in Germany* (March 15 and April 24, 1852), Collected Works, Vol. 11 pp.47, 71.

RACES AND NATIONS LESS FIT FOR PROGRESS AND CIVILISATION, "HISTORYLESS" PEOPLES, AND THE JUSTIFICATION OF CONQUEST AND COLONIALISM

"This splendid territory [Turkey in Europe] has the misfortune to be inhabited by a conglomerate of different races and nationalities, of which it is hard to say which is the least fit for progress and civilisation." Marx, "British Politics" (April 7, 1853), *Collected Works,* Vol. 12 p.7.

"And if during *eight centuries* the 'eight million Slavs' have had to suffer the yoke imposed on them by the four million Magyars, that alone sufficiently proves which was the more viable and vigorous, the many Slavs or the few Magyars! ... what a 'crime' it is, what a 'damnable policy' that at a time when, in Europe in general, big monarchies had become a 'historical necessity' , the Germans and Magyars united all these small, stunted and impotent little nations into a single big state and thereby enabled them to take part in a historical development from which, left to themselves, they would have remained completely aloof! Of course, matters of this kind cannot be accomplished without many a tender national bloom being forcibly broken. But in history nothing is achieved without violence and implacable ruthlessness, ... In short, it turns out these 'crimes' of the Germans and Magyars against the said Slavs are among the best and praiseworthy deeds which our and the Magyar people can boast of in their history." Engels, "Democratic Pan-Slavism" (*NRZ* February 15, 1849), *Collected Works,* Vol. 8 pp.370-71.

"These wretched, ruined fragments of one-time nations, the Serbs, Bulgars, Greeks and other robber bands, on behalf of which the liberal philistine waxes enthusiastic in the interests of Russia, are unwilling to grant each other the air they breathe, and feel obliged to cut each other's greedy throats...the lousy Balkan peoples...". Engels to August Bebel, November 17, 1885. Marx-Engels, *Briefe an A. Bebel, W. Liebknecht, K. Kautsky und Andere,* Moscow, 1933, pp.411, 412; translation by Bertram D. Wolfe, *Marxism, 1967, p.68.*

"Scandinavianism is enthusiasm for the brutal, sordid, piratical. Old Norse national traits, for that deep-rooted inner life which is unable to express its exuberant ideas and sentiments in words, but can express them only in deeds, namely in rudeness towards women, perpetual drunkeness and wild berserk frenzy alternating with tearful sentimentality." Engels, "The Danish-Prussian Armistice" (*NRZ* September 10, 1848), *Collected Works,* Vol. 7 p.422.

"The southern facile character of the Irishman, his crudity, which places him but little above the savage, his contempt for all humane enjoyments, in which his very crudeness makes him incapable of sharing, his filth and poverty, all favour drunkeness...the pressure of this race has done much to depress wages and lower the working-class...That poverty manifests itself in Ireland thus and not otherwise, is owing to the character of the people, and to their historical development. The Irish are a people related in their whole character to the Latin nations, to the French, and especially to the Italians... With the Irish, feeling and passion predominate; reason must bow before them. Their sensuous, excitable nature prevents reflection and quiet, persevering activity from reaching development - such a nation is utterly unfit for manufacture as now conducted ... Irish distress cannot be removed by any Act of Repeal. Such an Act would, however, at once lay bare the fact that the cause of Irish misery, which now seems to come from abroad, is really to be found at home." Engels, *The Condition of the Working-Class in England* (Authorised English edition of 1892. The book was first published in German in 1845). *Collected Works,* Vol. 4, pp.391-92, 559-61.

"It would seem as though history had first to make this whole people [the Chinese] drunk before it could rouse them from their hereditary stupidity". Marx, "Revolution in China and in Europe" (May 20, 1853), *Collected Works,* Vol. 12 p.94.

"... China, the rotting semi-civilization of the oldest State in the world ... Chinese nationality, with all its overbearing prejudice, stupidity, learned ignorance and pedantic barbarism ... Engels, "Persia and China" (June 5, 1857) in Marx-Engels, *On Colonialism,* Sixth Printing, Moscow, 1976, pp.120, 124.

"Peoples which have never had a history of their own, which from the time when they achieved the first, most elementary stage of civilisation already came under foreign sway, or which were *forced* to attain the first stage of civilisation only by means of a foreign yoke, are not viable and will never be able to achieve any kind of independence ... the Austrian Slavs have never had a history of their own, ...". Engels, "Democratic Pan-Slavism" (*NRZ* February 15 and 16, 1849), *Collected Works*, Vol. 8 pp. 367, 371.

"Indian society has no history at all, at least no known history ... The question, therefore, is not whether the English had a right to conquer India, but whether we are to prefer India conquered by the Turk, by the Persian, by the Russian, to India conquered by the Briton ... The British were the first conquerors superior, and therefore, inaccessible to Hindoo civilization." Marx, "The Future Results of British Rule in India" (July 22, 1853), *Collected Works*, Vol. 12 p. 218.

"By the same right under which France took Flanders, Lorraine and Alsace, and will sooner or later take Belgium - by that same right Germany takes over Schleswig; it is the right of civilization as against barbarism, of progress as against stability ... this right carries more weight than all the agreements, for it is the right of historical evolution." Engels, "The Danish - Prussian Armistice" (*NRZ* September 10, 1848), *Collected Works*, Vol. 7 p.423.

"... the conquest of Algeria is an important and fortunate fact for the progress of civilisation." Engels, "Abd-el-Kader" (January 22, 1848), *Collected Works*, Vol. 6 p.471. (This text is not included in the Soviet collection, Marx-Engels, *On Colonialism*, Sixth Printing, Moscow, 1976).

"In *America* we have witnessed the conquest of Mexico and have rejoiced at it. It is also an advance ... when such a country is forcibly drawn into the historical process. It is to the interest of its own development that Mexico will in future be placed under the tutelage of the United States. The evolution of the whole of America will profit by the fact that the United States, by the possession of California, obtains command of the Pacific." Engels, "The Movements of 1847" (January 23, 1848), *Collected Works*, Vol. 6 p. 527 (not in *On Colonialism*).

"And will Bakunin accuse the Americans of a 'war of conquest', which, although it deals a severe blow to his theory based on 'justice and humanity', was nevertheless waged wholly and solely in the interest of civilisation? Or is it perhaps unfortunate that splendid

California has been taken away from the lazy Mexicans, who could not do anything with it? ... The 'independence' of a few Spanish Californians and Texans may suffer because of it, in some places 'justice' and other moral principles may be violated; but what does that matter compared to such facts of world-historic significance?" Engels, "Democratic Pan-Slavism" (*NRZ* February 15, 1849), *Collected Works, Vol. 8, pp. 365-66.*

"England, it is true, in causing a social revolution in Hindostan, was actuated only by the vilest interests, and was stupid in her manner of enforcing them. But that is not the question. The question is, can mankind fulfil its destiny without a revolution in the social state of Asia? If not, whatever may have been the crimes of England she was the unconscious tool of history in bringing about that revolution." Marx, "The British Rule in India" (June 10, 1853), *Collected Works*, Vol. 12 p.132.

"Society is undergoing a silent revolution, which must be submitted to,... The classes and the races, too weak to master the new conditions of life, must give way." Marx, "Forced Emigration" (March 22, 1853), *Collected Works,* Vol. 11 p.531.

JEWS

"What is the secular basis of Judaism? *Practical* need, *self-interest.*

What is the worldly religion of the Jew? *Huckstering.* What is his worldly God? *Money* ...

We recognise in Judaism, therefore, a general *anti-social* element of the *present time,...*

Contempt for theory, art, history, and for man as an end in himself, which is contained in an abstract form in the Jewish religion, is the *real, conscious* standpoint, the virtue of the man of money...

The *chimerical* nationality of the Jew is the nationality of the merchant, of the man of money in general...

Once society has succeeded in abolishing the *empirical* essence of *Judaism* - huckstering and its preconditions - the Jew will have become *impossible, ...".* Marx, "On the Jewish Question" (1844), *Collected Works,* Vol. 3 pp. 169-74. (In *Karl Marx and the Radical Critique of Judaism,* Julius Carlebach has shown how little merit there is in the claim of some commentators that Marx's use of the terms "Jude" and "Judentum" in these essays is essentially devoid of religious and racial content).

"We discovered that in connection with these figures the German national simpletons and money-grubbers of the Frankfurt parliamentary swamp always counted as Germans the Polish Jews as well, although this meanest of all races, neither by its jargon nor by its descent, but at most only through its lust for profit, could have any relation of kinship with Frankfurt ... 'My glorious army' [the Prussian military] was let loose...in order in alliance with the Jews to plunder the churches, set fire to the villages, beat the Poles to death in public places with ramrods or brand them with caustic...". Engels, "[Posen]" (*NRZ* April 29, 1849), *Collected Works,* Vol. 9 pp. 359-60.

"... As a true Jew from the Slav frontier he [Lassalle] was always only too ready to exploit anyone for his private purposes under some party pretext. Then this eagerness to thrust himself into elegant society, to climb up, if only for appearance, to plaster over the grimy Breslau Jew with all kinds of pomade and make-up - all this was always repugnant." Engels to Marx, March 7, 1856. *The Marx-Engels Correspondence.* A selection edited by Fritz J. Raddatz, 1981, p. 71.

"Apropos Lassalle -Lazarus. In his *magnum opus* on Egypt, Lepsius has proved that the exodus of the Jews from Egypt was nothing other than the story Manetho relates of the expulsion from Egypt of 'the *leper* folk', with an Egyptian priest named Moses at their head. Lazarus the leper is thus the archetype of the Jew and of Lazarus - Lassalle." Letter from Marx to Engels, May 10, 1861. Marx-Engels, *Collected Works,* Vol. 41 (1985), p. 286. (In *Revolutionary Jews From Marx To Trotsky,* 1976, pp. 41-2, Robert S. Wistrich says that in this letter Marx managed to give credence to perhaps the oldest of the many legends invented against the Jews; the legend of the Jews as a 'leprous people' was a central theme in the pagan, pre-Christian literature of anti-Semitism.)

"The capitalist knows that all commodities, however scurvy they may look, or however badly they may smell, are in faith and in truth money, inwardly circumcised Jews, ...". Marx, *Capital* (1867), Vol. 1 Part II Chap. IV.

"Anti-Semitism is the characteristic sign of a backward civilisation and is therefore only found in Prussia and Austria or in Russia.... Anti-Semitism, therefore, is nothing but the reaction of the mediaeval, decadent strata of society against modern society, which essentially consists of wage-earners and capitalists; under a mask of apparent socialism it therefore only serves reactionary ends; it is a variety of feudal socialism and with that we can have nothing to do." Engels to an Unknown Correspondent, April 19, 1890. Marx-Engels, *Selected Correspondence,* London, 1943, pp. 469-471.

"The pettifogging business tricks of the Polish Jew, the representative in Europe of commerce in its lowest stage, those tricks that serve him so well in his own country, and are generally practised there, ...". Engels, *The Condition of the Working-Class in England,* Preface to the authorised English edition published in London in 1892. Moscow, 1973, pp.25-26.

"I begin to understand French anti-Semitism when I see how many Jews of Polish origin and with German names intrude themselves everywhere, arrogate everything to themselves and push themselves forward everywhere to the point of creating public opinion in the ville lumière, of which the Paris philistine is so proud and which he believes to be the supreme power in the universe." Engels to Paul Lafargue, July 22, 1892, in Frederick Engels, Paul and Laura Lafargue, *Correspondence,* Vol. III, Moscow, n.d. p.184.

BLACKS

"I mean direct slavery, the slavery of the Blacks in Surinam, in Brazil, in the southern regions of North America. ... Without slavery, North America, the most progressive nation would be transformed into a patriarchal country. Only wipe North America off the map and you will get anarchy, the complete decay of trade and modern civilization. But to do away with slavery would be to wipe America off the map...". Marx to P. V. Annenkov, December 28, 1846. *Collected Works,* Vol. 38 (1982), pp.101,102.

"The Jewish Nigger Lassalle,... fortunately departs at the end of this week, ... It is now completely clear to me that he, as is proved by his cranial formation and [curly] hair - descends from the Negroes who had joined Moses' exodus from Egypt (assuming his mother or grandmother on the paternal side had not interbred with a *nigger* [in English]. Now this union of Judaism and Germanism with a basic Negro substance must produce a peculiar product. The obtrusiveness of the fellow is also *Nigger*-like [in English]...One of the great discoveries of our Nigger [in English] - which he only confides to his 'most trusted friends' - is that the Pelasgians are descendants of the Semites." Marx to Engels, July 30, 1862. *The Letters of Karl Marx: Selected and Translated with Explanatory Notes and an Introduction* by Saul K. Padover (New Jersey, 1979) pp.466, 468. (This letter is not included in Marx-Engels, *Selected Correspondence,* but is in Marx-Engels, *Werke* (Berlin 1961-, Vol.30, pp. 257,259), the official East German edition of the collected works. The Soviet English-language edition of the *Selected Correspondence* published in New York in 1942 (p.vi) states: "With reference to the use of the word 'nigger' which occurs in this book: Marx used the word while living in England, in the last century. The word does not have the same connotation as it has now in the U.S. and should be read as 'Negro' whenever it occurs in the text." Diane Paul comments that "This explanation does not accord with that of the Oxford English Dictionary or with a great deal of other evidence. ... If the word 'nigger' was not so jarring in mid-nineteenth century England as it is in England or America today, it nevertheless was a term of abuse ... Both Marx and Engels sometimes used the English term 'nigger' to refer to blacks and to others for whom they had contempt...". (*Journal of the History of Ideas,* Jan-March 1981, pp. 126, 127).

"A very important work which I will send you...is: P. Trémaux, *Origin and Transformations of Man and Other Beings* (Paris, 1865)... In its historical and political application, the book is much more important and copious than Darwin. For certain questions, such as nationality, etc., a natural basis is found only in this work. For example, the author corrects the Pole Duchinski, ... just as he (he has been in Africa for a long time) proves that the common Negro type is only a degeneration of a much higher one: ...'The Slavic and Lithuanian races have, vis-à-vis the Muscovites, their real limit in the great geologic line which runs north of the Niemen and Dnieper basins... To the south of this great line, the abilities and the types typical of that region are and will always remain different from those of Russia.' " Marx to Engels, August 7, 1866. Saul K. Padover, *The Letters of Karl Marx,* 1979, pp.215-16. Marx-Engels, *Werke,* Vol. 31 pp. 248-49. (Not in Marx-Engels, *Selected Correspondence.* Marx's statement concerning the "degenerate" Negro type is also omitted in the Soviet account ("Marx and Engels on Biology") by V. L. Komarov in N.I. Bukharin et al., *Marxism and Modern Thought,* 1935, pp.194-95).

"I have arrived at the conviction that there is nothing to his [Trémaux's] theory if for no other reason than because he neither understands geology nor is capable of the most ordinary literary historical criticism. One could laugh oneself sick about his stories of the nigger Santa Maria and of the transmutations of the whites into Negroes. Especially, that the traditions of the Senegal niggers deserve absolute credulity, just because the rascals cannot write!...Perhaps this man will prove in the second volume, how he explains the fact, that we Rhinelanders have not long ago turned into idiots and niggers on our own Devonian Transition rocks... Or perhaps he will maintain that we are real niggers." Letter from Engels to Marx, October 2, 1866. Quoted by Diane Paul, " 'In the Interests of Civilization': Marxist Views of Race and Culture in the Nineteenth Century", *Journal of the History of Ideas,* Jan-March 1981, p.123. [*Werke,* Vol. 31, p. 256.]

"Lafargue has the usual stigma of the Negro tribe: *no sense of shame,* I mean thereby no modesty about making himself ridiculous." Marx to Engels, November 11, 1882. Saul K. Padover, *The Letters of Karl Marx,* 1979, p.399.

Marx's second daughter, Laura, married Paul Lafargue who, Engels said, had "one eighth or one twelfth Nigger blood". In 1887, Paul was a candidate for the Paris Municipal Council, in a district which contained the Jardin des Plantes and the Zoo. In a letter to Laura (April 26, 1887), Engels referred to "Paul, the candidate of the Jardin des Plantes - and the animals" and added: "Being in his quality as a nigger a degree nearer to the rest of the animal kingdom than the rest of us, he is undoubtedly the most appropriate representative of that district." (Frederick Engels, Paul and Laura Lafargue, *Correspondence,* Vol. II, Moscow, 1960, p.37. Marx-Engels, *Werke,* Vol. 36 (1967), p.645.) Reference to Lafargue's "Nigger blood" is made in a letter from Engels to F.A. Sorge (November 14, 1891), *Werke,* Vol. 38.

WAR

"Such is the redeeming feature of war ; it puts a nation to the test. As exposure to the atmosphere reduces all mummies to instant dissolution, so war passes supreme judgment upon social organisations that have outlived their vitality." Marx, "Another British Revelation" (September 24, 1855), *Collected Works,* Vol. 14 p.516.

"Only a *war against Russia* would be a war of *revolutionary Germany,* a war by which she could cleanse herself of her past sins, could take courage, defeat her own autocrats, spread civilisation by the sacrifice of her own sons...". ("German Foreign Policy and the Latest Events in Prague", in *NRZ* July 12, 1848, *Collected Works,* Vol. 7, p.212. Many of the *NRZ* articles seem to be the joint work of Marx and Engels, and it has not so far proved possible to ascertain which one of them wrote this particular item.)

"The French need a thrashing. If the Prussians win, centralisation of the state power will be useful for the centralisation of the German working class. German predominance would also transfer the centre of gravity of the workers' movement in Western Europe from France to Germany, and one has only to compare the movement in the two countries from 1866 till now to see that the German working class is superior to the French both theoretically and organisationally. Their predominance over the French on the world stage would also mean the predominance of *our* theory over Proudhon's, etc." Marx to Engels, July 20, 1870. Marx-Engels, *Selected Correspondence,* London, 1943, p.292. (This letter is excluded from Marx-Engels, *Selected Correspondence,* Third revised edition, Moscow, 1975.)

"If the fortune of her arms, the arrogance of success, and dynastic intrigue lead Germany to a dismemberment of France, there will then only remain two courses open to her. She must at all risks become the *avowed* tool of Russian aggrandizement or, after some short respite, make again ready for another 'defensive' war, not one of those new-fangled 'localized' wars, but a *war of races* - a war with the combined Slavonian and Roman races." Second Address of the

General Council of the International Working Men's Association on the Franco-Prussian War. Written by Marx September 9, 1870. Marx-Engels, *Selected Works,* Moscow, 1958, Vol. 1 p.495.

"... no war is any longer possible for Prussia-Germany except a world war and a world war indeed of an extension and violence hitherto undreamt of. Eight to ten millions of soldiers will mutually massacre one another and in doing so devour the whole of Europe until they have stripped it barer than any swarm of locusts has ever done. The devastations of the Thirty Years' War compressed into three or four years, and spread over the whole continent; famine, pestilence, general demoralisation both of the armies and of the mass of the people produced by acute distress; hopeless confusion of our artificial machinery in trade, industry and credit, ending in general bankruptcy;... only one result absolutely certain: general exhaustion and the establishment of the conditions for the ultimate victory of the working class.... This, my lords, princes and statesmen, is where in your wisdom you have brought old Europe. And when nothing more remains to you but to open the last great war dance - that will suit us all right." From Engels's introduction to the reissue (1887) of a pamphlet by Sigismund Borkheim. Marx-Engels, *Selected Correspondence,* London, 1943, pp.456-57. (Not in *Selected Correspondence,* Third revised edition, Moscow, 1975.)

"... if war is forced upon us, and moreover a war in alliance with *Russia,* we must regard this as an attack on our existence and defend ourselves by every method, utilising all positions at our disposal and therefore Metz and Strasbourg also ... so our army will have to lead and sustain the main push ... So much seems certain to me: if we are beaten, every barrier to chauvinism and a war of revenge in Europe will be thrown down for years hence. If we are victorious our Party will come into power. The victory of Germany is therefore the victory of the revolution, and if it comes to war we must not only desire victory but further it by every means." Engels to Bebel, September 29, 1891. Marx-Engels, *Selected Correspondence,* London, 1943, pp.489-90. (Not in *Selected Correspondence,* Third revised edition, Moscow, 1975.)

"... if France and Russia in alliance attacked Germany, the last-named would defend to the death her national existence, in which the German Socialists are even more interested than the bourgeois. The

Socialists would thus fight to the last man and would not hesitate to resort to the revolutionary means employed by France in 1793." (Interview with Engels published in the Paris daily paper *L'Éclair* of April 6th, 1892, in Frederick Engels, Paul and Laura Lafargue, *Correspondence,* Vol. III, Moscow,n.d., pp. 387-88. The text of this interview was "almost entirely recast" by Engels before publication.)

APPENDIX II

MARX AND DARWIN

THE UNVEILING OF A MYTH

LESLIE R. PAGE

First published June 1983

ISBN 0 948316 01 2

Marx and Darwin
The Unveiling of a Myth

1. The Marx-Darwin Dedication Story and its Unravelling

In 1983 a book with the title *Marxism and Anthropology* was published as part of a series of *Marxist Introductions* edited by Raymond Williams and Steven Lukes. On page 5, the author, Maurice Bloch, who is a Reader in Anthropology in the University of London, states: "Indeed Marx saw his work very much in this light and at one time proposed to dedicate *Capital* to Darwin, who refused, horrified as he already was by the religious and political repercussions of what he had written." In an article titled "Survival of the Fittest Philosophy" (*New Socialist*, July/August 1982), Steven Rose, a Professor of biology at the Open University likewise declares that "Marx wanted to dedicate *Capital* to Darwin." And Stephen Jay Gould, a Professor of biology, geology, and the history of science at Harvard University, to whom Rose refers in his article, is also among those who have given this Marx-Darwin dedication story the blessing of historical fact. Gould relates it with equal certainty and in some detail in the 1978 edition of his book "Ever Since Darwin" - although he has since published a retraction. Gould, it may be noted, says he "learned his Marxism, literally at his daddy's knee", whilst Rose and his co-authors invoke "the understanding of Marxist philosophers like Georg Lukács and Agnes Heller and of revolutionary practitioners and theorists like Mao Tse Tung."[1]

It is, in fact, completely untrue that Karl Marx tried to dedicate some part of *Capital* to Charles Darwin, as the researches - first published in 1975 and 1976 - of Lewis S. Feuer and others, and the discovery, in 1975, of definitive evidence, have shown.[2] The myth of an intellectual affinity between Marx and Darwin, disseminated by Marxists as evidence for their theory's "scientific" status, seemed to be given credibility and support by the publication, in 1931, in a Soviet journal, of a Russian translation of a letter written by Darwin on October 13, 1880. The Marx-Engels Institute in Moscow - which described this letter as a "Letter of Charles Darwin to Karl Marx" - was responsible for promulgating the myth that Marx wanted to dedicate part of *Capital* to Darwin. In a short Introduction - marked, says Ralph Colp, Jr. "by ignorance and ineptitudes" - the Institute declared that the letter was "Darwin's answer to Marx's request to look over the proof-sheets of the English edition of *Das Kapital* ... where Marx refers to the evolutionary doctrine." Darwin, it was stated, "declined the honour of having corresponding chapters dedicated to him, being apprehensive that he should be suspected of approving the work defaming the middle classes."

In 1934, a Soviet year-by-year chronology of Marx's life, compiled by the Marx-Engels-Lenin Institute in Moscow, was published in Russian and German. An entry for the beginning of October, 1880, giving as its source Darwin's letter of 13 October 1880, states: "Marx requests Darwin by letter to accept the dedication of the second volume of *Capital;* Darwin refuses on the grounds (among others) that he did not want to hurt the religious feelings of his family." The massive collective work, *Karl Marx: a biography,* issued in 1973 by the Institute for Marxism-Leninism in Moscow continued to describe (p.321) how Darwin declined to accept a dedication by Marx, though it did not specify clearly what dedication. And in the same year, the Marx scholar, David McLellan, wrote that "Marx certainly wished to dedicate the Second Volume of *Capital* to Darwin" but "Darwin refused the honour, ...". *(Karl Marx: His Life and Thought,* p.424; unchanged in the latest reprint in 1983). And again, in an article on Marx and Darwin in *New Left Review* (November-December 1973), the Communist philosopher Valentino Gerratana asserted that "In 1880, in fact, Marx asked Darwin by letter for permission to dedicate Volume II of *Capital* to him".

But as Margaret A. Fay has commented, the scholarly consensus was strangely silent about Engels' testimony to the contrary in his Preface to the first German edition of *Capital,* Volume II. Engels declared that "The second and third books of *Capital* were to be dedicated, as Marx had stated repeatedly, to his wife." Added to which, there were a number of other reasons for questioning the Marx-Darwin dedication story. In *Ever Since Darwin* (Pelican Books, 1980, Reprinted 1981, pp.26-27), Gould retracts assertions he made in the 1978 edition that "Marx later offered to dedicate Volume 2 of *Das Kapital* to Darwin, but Darwin gently declined, ...", adding in the later edition: "But Marx and Darwin did correspond , and Marx held Darwin in very high regard." Gould then quotes a part of Darwin's letter of 13 October 1880 but does not say to whom Darwin was writing. So what was the history of the Marx-Darwin myth?

On 16 June 1873 Marx sent Darwin an inscribed copy of the recently published second German edition of *Das Kapital*, Volume 1, and on the same day (according to the Soviet chronology of Marx's life, p.345) he also sent a copy to Herbert Spencer. From Darwin, three and a half months after receiving his copy, came a short acknowledgement letter in two sentences, dated October 1, 1873. Although Marx and Darwin each lived for another decade and only a few miles apart, that was in fact the beginning and the end of their correspondence, and they never met. Darwin's letter, says Colp, implies "that he does not want to discuss Marx's book or have any further contact with its author."

Darwin's letter of 13 October 1880 was not a letter to Marx at all. It was sent not to Marx but to Edward B. Aveling who became the lover of Marx's daughter Eleanor and, with her, had access to Marx's papers which they sorted through and prepared what they could for publication, after the death of Engels in 1895. The "Part or Volume" to which Darwin had referred in his letter was not Volume II of *Capital* but Aveling's handbook *The Student's Darwin* which was published in 1881 and was the second volume in a series of works on Science & Freethought. The definitive evidence that Aveling was the recipient of Darwin's letter was the discovery, in 1975, of a letter written by Aveling and dated October 12, 1880, in a collection of Darwin's papers in Cambridge University Library. Darwin's letter of 13 October 1880 was a reply to Aveling's letter of 12 October 1880 in which Aveling requested permission to dedicate *The Student's Darwin* to Darwin. Marx never tried to dedicate any of his work to Darwin. Copies of Aveling's letter were shown in 1975 to members of the Moscow Institute of the History of Natural Sciences. In 1977, Colp adds, an article was published in the Soviet journal *Priroda* relating how the myth of Marx wanting to dedicate *Capital* to Darwin began in 1931 and how the letter of Aveling refuted the myth. The Institute of Marxism-Leninism approved this publication.

As Professor Feuer indicates, it seems strange that during a period when so many Western scientists and historians of science were drawn to Marxism, not a single scholar or scientist undertook to test the purported Marx-Darwin connection by the usual methods of critical scholarship. The many scholars, Communist scientists, historians of science, and fellow-travelling enquirers who were misled by the uncritical Soviet publication of 1931, failed, says Feuer, to exercise that critical judgment in the testing of hypotheses which they otherwise customarily used. Doubts about what was proclaimed to be Marx's offer of dedication were, however, raised in 1959 by Conway Zirkle [3], an American botanist and historian of biological ideas, and several years later, by the political scientist Shlomo Avineri. [4]

As Avineri showed, the linking of Marx's name with that of Darwin derived from a calculated literary hoax perpetrated by Marx and Engels on the editor of a provincial German newspaper. In his funeral oration at the graveside of Karl Marx in 1883, Friedrich Engels declared that: "Just as Darwin discovered the law of development of organic nature, so Marx discovered the law of development of human history." Gerratana, in his article on Marx and Darwin, says that "This verdict of Engels on the fundamental parallelism between Marx and Darwin was later taken up again and again, and eventually became a commonplace of Marxist literature." In 1894, Lenin, referring to Marx's *Capital,* asserted that "It will now be clear that the comparison with Darwin is perfectly accurate." [5] In 1895, Plekhanov wrote that "one can say that Marxism is Darwinism in its application to social science." [6] And in 1968 in *The Open Philosophy and the Open Society* the communist Maurice Cornforth said (p.27): "The methodology by which Marx arrived at his theory of social development is exactly the same as that employed by Darwin in establishing the theory of evolution of species by natural selection. Engels in fact remarked on this in his speech at Marx's funeral ...". But what was the origin of Engels's simile between Marx and Darwin? And what was Marx's real opinion of the greatest biological scientist of his age?

When the first volume of *Das Kaptial* was published in September 1867 Marx was anxious to obtain publicity for his work. In letters to Engels and to Dr. Kugelmann (October 10 and 11, 1867), Marx urged on his friends the publication of reviews of his book emphasising that immediate success is not the result of "genuine criticism" and "it is not very important *what is said*", but that what matters is "creating a stir...beating the drum". [7] Engels wrote a number of reviews of *Das Kapital* "from different points of view" and "from a bourgeois standpoint" and Marx told Engels (8 Jan. 1868): "Jenny [Marx's eldest daughter], a specialist in these matters, asserts that you have developed a great dramatic and even a comic talent in this matter of 'different points of view' and various disguises". [8]

In a letter to Engels dated 7 November 1867, Marx referred to *Das Kapital* - "this first attempt at applying the *dialectic method* to Political Economy", saying that there was a great necessity to know the dialectical method and perhaps this was the easiest way to attract the English people.[9] Yet only a month later, again writing to Engels, Marx made no mention of the dialectic method or any comparison of his work with that of Hegel, but compared his work with that of Darwin, in an endeavour to attract the interest of prospective readers. Marx specified how Engels should review *Das Kapital* to make it seem palatable to a German liberal newspaper, *Der Beobachter,* published in Stuttgart. Marx had made enquiries about the paper and found out that its editor, Karl Mayer, was an enthusiastic Darwinist who believed in the natural superiority of laisser-faire. He was also a friend of the natural scientist Karl Vogt with whom Marx had been involved in a bitter quarrel. In his letter of 7 December 1867 - usually omitted in "official" Marxist collections - Marx told Engels that "it would be an amusing coup to swindle Vogt's friend..." and he directed Engels in the course of his review to write: "... one has to distinguish between the positive description given by the author and the tendentious conclusions drawn by him ... When he [Marx] proves that contemporary society, economically considered, is pregnant with a new, higher form, then he only shows socially the same universal process of change which was proved in the natural sciences by Darwin. The liberal doctrine of 'Progress' (that's Mayer tout pur) implies this,...".

Under this disguise, the review was printed. Engels carried out Marx's instructions and the review - which is not included in the Soviet collection, Engels: *On Marx's Capital,* 1976 - was duly published in *Der Beobachter* of 27 December 1867.[10] Marx and Engels realised that it would be expedient to link Marx's name with that of Darwin and induce the reading public to imagine that Marx was carrying out in sociology and history the same sort of revolutionary scientific work that Darwin had already achieved in biology. "The concept of 'the scientific method' ", the Soviet mathematician Igor Shafarevich observes, "was of extraordinary importance for the development of nineteenth-century socialism ... the theses of socialist doctrine thereby acquired the appearance of objectivity and a certain inevitability,....". "Marx himself ", says David McLellan, "called his work scientific (so did Hegel), but in his work the term had much less the connotation of natural scientific methodology".[11]

2.The Impact of Darwin and Marx's Disenchantment

When *The Origin of Species* appeared on 24 November 1859, it was sold out on the first day of publication and Engels immediately grasped its importance and wrote to Marx on 11 or 12 December 1859 (*Werke*, Vol. 29, p.524): "Darwin whom I am just now reading is quite splendid. Teleology in one respect had not hitherto been finished off: it is now. Never yet has such a magnificent attempt been made to demonstrate historical development in nature or at least with such success. Of course, one must put up with the crude English method". But it was about a year later - in a letter to Engels dated 19 December 1860 - before Marx referred to having read Darwin's book. At first, Marx gave it qualified approval, although he was not quite so enthusiastic as Engels. In a letter to F. Lassalle (16 January 1861) Marx said that Darwin's work "serves me as a natural-scientific basis for the class struggle in history ... Despite all deficiencies, not only is the death-blow dealt here for the first time to 'teleology' in the natural sciences, but its rational meaning is empirically explained". But Marx's judgment - like that of Engels - was tempered by a reservation about Darwin's "crude English method".[12] It is a pity, remarks Grace Carlton in her book on Engels,[13] that Marx could not prevail on himself to employ the same method.

Darwin had spent over twenty years in observation and experimentation and in collecting and investigating the facts on which his evolutionary theory rested, and his empirical method evoked admiration for its "scrupulous, careful, thorough and fair-minded marshalling of evidences". It was, said Thomas Huxley, "a piece of critical self-discipline which saved him [Darwin] from endless errors of detail". Marx, for his part, had become a communist, before his twenty-sixth birthday and at a very early stage in his career, largely under the influence of German philosophers, particularly Hegel.[14] He formed his viewpoint first, and then went through whole libraries to find "scientific verification" of his pre-existing theory of communism[15] which he had already asserted, in 1844, "is the solution to the riddle of history and knows itself to be this solution".[16] As Emile Durkheim wrote in reference to Marx's *Capital*: "The researches ... were undertaken to establish a doctrine ... previously conceived, rather than the doctrine being a result of the research".[17]

While Marx and Engels praised Darwin for eliminating "teleology" (the metaphysical principle of design or purposefulness) from the natural sciences, they retained a teleological element in their own theories and dialectical laws. In Chapter XI of the first edition of *The Origin of Species* Darwin said: "I believe, as was remarked in the last chapter, in no law of necessary development". And at least twice in each edition of *The Origin of Species* Darwin asserts the independence of natural selection from any 'necessary', 'universal', or 'fixed' law of progressive development.[18] But Marx wrote of "the expression of a necessary development," of "a development...through the very nature of things", of "the laws of appropriation or of private property" which "become by their own inner and inexorable dialectic changed into their very opposite". "It is a question", Marx declared, "of these laws themselves, of these tendencies working with iron necessity towards inevitable results. ... Capitalist production begets with the inexorability of a law of nature its own negation. It is the negation of negation".[19]

In fact, however, as Allen E. Buchanan[20] points out, Marx does not even attempt to show how the phases of communism with their specific characteristics, which he describes in his *Critique of the Gotha Programme,* can be predicted on the basis of definite features of his analysis of the "laws of motion of capitalism" in *Capital.* As Z.A. Jordan[21] says, "*Capital* could not and did not validate the hypothesis concerning the necessity of its replacement by a socialist formation into which the capitalist mode of production must inevitably pass over ... A hypothesis may be enlightening, interesting, and fruitful without being a law; Darwin's conjecture concerning the origin of species is an instance in point".

"In Marx's dialectic of history no less than in Hegel's", writes the anthropologist Marvin Harris,[22] "each epoch or social formation is urged onward towards its inevitable negation by an uncanny teleological thrust". And M.M. Bober, in his excellent study (*Karl Marx's Interpretation of History*), remarks that Marx and Engels "do not demonstrate how Darwin can be brought into explicit accord with the dialectic ... the impression can scarcely be escaped that there dwells in Marx's and Engels' dialectic an element of mysticism. ... Whether Marx intended it to be so or not, the dialectic often serves as a respectable authentication of propositions insufficiently demonstrated".[23] Marx himself says, in regard to the use of dialectics, in a letter to Engels, quoted by Shafarevich (op.cit. p.210): "I took the risk of prognosticating in this way, as I was compelled to substitute for you as correspondent at the *Tribune*. Nota bene - on the supposition that the dispatches we have got up till now are correct. It is possible that I may be discredited. But in that case it will still be possible to pull through with the help of a bit of dialectics. It goes without saying that I phrased my forecasts in such a way that I would prove to be right also in the opposite case". This letter dated 15 August, 1857 is in Marx-Engels *Werke* (Berlin: Vol. 29, 1963, pp.160-61).

In 1862 Marx re-read Darwin and formed a rather different opinion of his work. In a letter to Engels (18 June 1862) Marx sought to reduce Darwin's scientific significance to an "ideological" projection of bourgeois society upon the plant and animal world. "Darwin", he said, "whom I have looked up again, amuses me when he says that he is applying the 'Malthusian' theory to plants and animals *also,* whereas the whole point of Mr Malthus lies in the fact that he does *not* apply his theory to plants and animals, but only to human beings - and with geometrical progression - as opposed to plants and animals. It is remarkable how Darwin recognizes among beasts and plants his English society with its division of labour, competition, opening up of new markets, 'inventions', and the Malthusian 'struggle for existence'. It is Hobbes's *bellum omnium contra omnes,* and one is reminded of Hegel's *Phenomenology,* where civil society is described as a 'spiritual animal kingdom', while in Darwin the animal kingdom figures as civil society...".

Gerratana quotes these comments of Marx and, in discussing Darwin's reference to Malthus's *Essay On the Principle of Population,* asserts that "none of the later interpreters of Darwin took the trouble to check the original texts, which are nevertheless well-known and easily accessible, to establish the exact value of Darwin's reference". This is simply not true of Conway Zirkle whose work Gerratana does not mention. Some years before Gerratana wrote his article, Zirkle, a Professor of botany, checked the texts - lengthy extracts from which he reproduced - and recorded Malthus's contribution to the thinking of Darwin and Wallace, and the misrepresentation of Malthus by Marx and Engels. And whereas Gerratana (as well as Sebastiano Timpanaro, in his book *On Materialism,* pp. 41 and 85) unequivocally endorsed the myth of the Marx-Darwin dedication, Zirkle, writing in 1959, referred to it, in passing, preceded by the words: "As the story goes...".

In his book, *Evolution, Marxian Biology and the Social Scene,* Zirkle examined the extract from Marx's letter to Engels of 18 June, 1862 quoted above, as well as similar or related passages in a number of other letters and works of Marx, Engels, Malthus, Komarov, Lysenko, et al. Zirkle states (pp. 88, 89, 359) that "If Marx had really read Malthus, we would be forced to conclude either that he did not understand what he had read or that he had knowingly misrepresented what Malthus had written ... In his letter to Engels of June 18, 1862, he made the misstatement '... whereas the whole point of Mr Malthus lies in the fact that he does not apply his theory to plants and animals but only to man - with geometric progression - as opposed to plants and animals.' Malthus, of course, had applied his geometrical progression to the entire animal and plant kingdom, ... if Marx had been familiar with the very first chapter of Malthus' *Essay* (2nd Ed., 1803, and all subsequent editions) he would have found the following passage: 'The cause to which I allude is the constant tendency of all animated life to increase beyond the nourishment prepared for it. ... This is incontrovertibly true. Throughout the animal and vegetable kingdoms Nature has scattered the seeds of life abroad with the most profuse and liberal hand, but has been comparatively sparing in the room and nourishment necessary to rear them. The germs of existence contained in this earth, if they could freely develop themselves, would fill millions of worlds in the course of a few thousand years. Necessity, that imperious, all-pervading law of nature, restrains them within the prescribed bounds. The race of plants and the race of animals shrink under this great restrictive law; and man cannot by any efforts of reason escape from it'."[24]

As for Marx being "compelled to say", as Komarov[25] puts it, "that Darwin was transferring to plants and animals the peculiarities of the English capitalist system" - Hobbes's *bellum omnium contra omnes* (war of all against all), Marx himself, in Volume 1 of *Capital* (Chap. XIV, Section 4), stated that: "The division of labour within the society brings into contact independent commodity producers, who acknowledge no other authority but that of competition, of the coercion exerted by the pressure of their mutual interests; just as in the animal kingdom, the bellum omnium contra omnes more or less preserves the conditions of existence of every species." And in fact, comments C. Bouglé, in his essay "Darwinism and Sociology":[26] "He [Darwin] never insisted, like his rival, Wallace, upon the necessity of the solitary struggle of creatures in a state of nature, each for himself and against all. On the contrary, in *The Descent of Man,* he pointed out the serviceableness of the social instincts ...". As has also been indicated by Enrico Ferri,[27] Hobbes's "Warre of every one against every one" - invoked by Marx in relation to "civil society" - was conceived by Hobbes as applying, not to "civil society", but to "the naturall condition of mankind, ... before the time of Civill Society, or in the interruption thereof by Warre." (Hobbes, *Leviathan,* Part 1, Chap. XIV).

In his *Theories of Surplus Value* [Volume IV of *Capital*] written between January 1862 and July 1863, Marx, says Zirkle, repeated his misstatement about Malthus: "In his excellent work, Darwin did not see that his discovery of the 'geometrical' progression in the animal and vegetable kingdoms overturns Malthus's theory ...". A few pages earlier, Marx, in another passage gives some further indication of the relationship between his work and that of Darwin: "Apart from the barrenness of such edifying reflections [by Sismondi], they reveal a failure to understand the fact that that although at first the development of the capacities of the *human* species takes place at the cost of the majority of human individuals and even classes, in the end it breaks through this contradiction and coincides with the development of the individual; the higher development of individuality is thus only achieved by a historical process during which individuals are sacrificed, for the interests of the species in the human kingdom, as in the animal and plant kingdoms, always assert themselves at the cost of the interests of individuals, because these interests of the species coincide only with the *interests of certain individuals,* and it is this coincidence which constitutes the strength of these privileged individuals."[28]

In this passage a parallel is drawn between the historical development of the human species (which takes place at the expense of individuals) and that of animals and plants, and, Marx adds, human development will finally break down the antagonism between individual and species. As Enrique Ureña says, the Marxian interpretation of history does not stop at the class struggle.[29] Marx wanted to show scientifically that this struggle would necessarily lead to communist society, and he desired to find a basis in natural science in accord with his political and social concepts. Marx and Engels, Zirkle concludes, accepted only those parts of the biology of their time which were compatible with their social and economic doctrines (op.cit., p.353).

3.Race and Culture: Marx or Darwin?

On 7 August, 1866 Marx wrote to Engels with an intense enthusiasm - which contrasted with the qualified praise he had bestowed upon Darwin - about an exciting discovery he had made of a book by Pierre Trémaux,[30] a French traveller and amateur ethnologist, who claimed to have revealed the interrelationships between soils, races, and human evolution. Trémaux adopted an extreme environmentalist approach and announced "The Great Law of the Perfecting of Beings". This was that the beauty, energy, level of civilization, and intellectual faculties of peoples and races were, in general, related directly to the geological age of the soil on which they lived. Marx's environmentalist bias and his real opinion of Darwin were demonstrated when he hailed Trémaux's work, in spite of all deficiencies, as "a very important advance over Darwin. The two chief arguments are: that cross-breeding does not produce differences, as one believes, but on the contrary it produces the typical unity of the species. The earth's crust causes the differences (not by itself but as their chief basis). Progress, which is pure chance with Darwin, is here a necessity on the basis of the developmental periods of the earth; ...".

In another paragraph of his letter to Engels, Marx wrote that: "In its historical and political application, the book is much more important and copious than Darwin. For certain questions, such as nationality, etc., a natural basis is found only in this work." According to Marx, Trémaux had proved "that the common Negro type is only a degeneration of a much higher one ... 'The same nature, the same abilities, will be reborn on the same soil. ... The Slavic and Lithuanian races have, vis-à-vis the Muscovites, their real limit in the great geologic line which runs north of the Niemen and Dnieper basins ... To the south of this great line, the abilities and the types typical of that region are and will always remain different from those of Russia'."

Trémaux had, indeed, proclaimed that: "The backward Negro is not a perfected ape, but a degenerated human being." Nathaniel Weyl describes Trémaux as a "racist crackpot" and says: "That Marx could actually believe that a quack like Trémaux was a greater scientist than Darwin was a measure of his incapacity to understand either science or scientific method." It is easy to understand, says Zirkle, why, in modern Communist accounts of the biology of Marx and Engels, the whole Trémaux affair is either slurred over or ignored.

At all events, Engels replied to Marx on 2 October, 1866 saying that whilst he had not finished reading the book he had arrived at the conviction that Trémaux did not understand geology, that his stories were laughable, and his book was "not worth anything, a pure fabrication, which defies all facts ...". "Perhaps," said Engels, "this man will prove in the second volume, how he explains the fact, that we Rhinelanders have not long ago turned into idiots and niggers on our own Devonian Transition rocks ... Or perhaps he will maintain that we are real niggers."

Marx immediately wrote Engels a rejoinder (3 October, 1866) stating that: "Trémaux's basic idea on the influence of the soil is, in my opinion, an idea which needs only to be announced to earn for itself an eternal citizenship in the sciences and, at that, entirely independent of Trémaux's presentation." Two days later, Engels wrote back saying that he had now finished reading Trémaux's book and tempering his adverse comments a little: "This man has the distinction of having stressed the influence of the soil upon racial and, logically, species formation more than has happened so far. And secondly, of having developed more correct opinions on the effect of crossing than his predecessors (though in my opinion very one-sided ones). Darwin, in *one* sense, is also right in his ideas on the transmuting influence of crossing;... Also, Darwin and others have never failed to recognize the influence of the soil. And if it happened that they did not stress it especially it was because they knew nothing about it ... And Trémaux does not know much more either. There is something tremendously plausible about the hypothesis that the soil becomes in general more favourable for the development of higher species in proportion to its belonging to newer formations. This hypothesis may or may not be correct ...". To this, Marx made no reply and there was no further mention of Trémaux in the correspondence between Marx and Engels. But on 9 October, 1866 Marx wrote to the surgeon and gynaecologist Dr L. Kugelmann commending Trémaux's book and reiterating his original opinion that, despite deficiencies, "it is still - for all that and all that - an advance on Darwin." Trémaux's theory is now forgotten and disappeared virtually without a trace in the history of biological science.

In his substantial volume, *Karl Marx: His Life and Thought,* David McLellan makes no mention of Trémaux although on pages 423-4 he quotes two phrases from Marx's letter concerning Trémaux which

Marx sent to Engels on 7 August, 1866. The Index of Names in *The Ethnological Notebooks of Karl Marx* (1972), edited by Lawrence Krader, gives one reference to Trémaux and in one short sentence in one of the 182 notes to the text of his Introduction, Krader says simply: "Here the work of Trémaux is advanced over that of Darwin."[31]

Marx and Engels evidently believed in racial differences. In *Capital*, Trémaux is not mentioned but Marx refers in Volume 1 (Part V Chap. XVI) to "the constitution of man himself (race etc.)", and in Volume 3 (Chap. XLVII) to "inborn racial characteristics". In *The German Ideology*, Marx and Engels declare that "Even naturally evolved differences within the species, such as racial differences, etc. ... can and must be abolished in the course of historical development," although they do not suggest how rapidly this might occur. And when Marx and Engels referred to actual races, nations, and people, as opposed to general, theoretical pronouncements on Race, national differences, and Communism, they were not above expressions of hatred or contempt, and were ready to justify war and conquest, terror, and domination of the lesser and more "barbaric" breeds of the human family by the peoples of Germanic or West European origin. Both Marx and Engels have, in fact, been indicted for racist or anti-semitic propensities as evidenced by their characterization of the Slavs, Jews, Blacks, and others. Silberner (1949), Zirkle (1959), Carlos Moore (1972), Chaloner and Henderson (1975), and Weyl (1979) are among those who have made and documented such charges.[32]

Belief in a hierarchy of cultures with their own at the top was common among nineteenth-century Europeans. In a letter to William Graham (3 July 1881), less than a year before his death, Darwin wrote: "... The more civilized so-called Caucasian races have beaten the Turkish hollow in the struggle for existence. Looking to the world at no very distant date, what an endless number of the lower races will have been eliminated by the higher civilized races throughout the world." But we should not therefore rush to brand Darwin as a "racist", says John C. Greene in an article on "Darwin as a Social Evolutionist".[33] If, as seems clear, Darwin shared the belief of most of his contemporaries in the existence of racial differences, "he did so because he thought the evidence seemed to require it, and he qualified his statements in cases where the evidence seemed contradictory, as in the case of the moral differences 'believed to exist' between human races. Ever the cautious scientist, Darwin was much more reserved and open-minded in his judgements on the heritability of acquired characters, the superior talents of the Anglo-Saxon peoples, and the role of natural selection in history than were most of the writers whose works he read and annotated. Above all, he was careful to recognize 'the obligations of enlightened humanity' toward the peoples of every nation and race ... people must obey the promptings of their sympathetic impulses, for these, too, were products of the evolutionary process." Darwin denounced the "great crime" of Slavery, recording in one of his notebooks: "Has not the white man, who has debased his nature by making slave of his fellow Black, often wished to consider him as other animal." And, referring to Argentina, he said it "will be in the hands of white Gaucho savages instead of copper coloured Indians, the former being a little superior in civilization, as they are inferior in every moral virtue".[34]

Marx said of Negro slavery: "Without slavery, North America, the most progressive nation would be transformed into a patriarchal country. Only wipe North America off the map and you will get anarchy, the complete decay of trade and modern civilization. But to do away with slavery would be to wipe America off the map ...."[35]

In Volume 1 of *Capital* Marx criticised Malthus in several footnotes but did not connect him with Darwin. In Chapter X, Section 5, Marx refers to natural selection without, however, mentioning Darwin. He writes: "And, indeed, experience shows to the intelligent observer with what swiftness and grip the capitalist mode of production ... has seized the vital power of the people by the very root - ... shows how even the country labourers, in spite of fresh air and the principle of natural selection, that works so powerfully amongst them, and only permits the survival of the strongest, are already beginning to die off." As the first volume of *Capital* was going to press, Marx, says Colp, hurriedly added two footnotes referring to Darwin. In Chapter XIV, Section 2, where Marx discusses the modern development of specialised tools, he inserts a footnote referring to Darwin's "epoch-making work" and quotes from the *Origin of Species* some remarks of Darwin with reference to the natural organs of plants and animals. In the second footnote (Chapter XV, Section 1), in discussing the difference between tools and machines, Marx says that "Darwin has interested us in the history of Nature's Technology, i.e. in the formation of the organs of plants and animals, ... Does not the history of the productive organs of man, ... deserve equal attention? ... human history differs from natural history in this, that we have made the former, but not the latter. ... The weak points in the abstract materialism of natural science, a materialism that excludes history and its process, are at once evident from the abstract and ideological conceptions of its spokesmen whenever they venture beyond the bounds of their own speciality."

As Bouglé observes, the very importance Marx and Engels attach to tools and machines proves that they were not likely to forget the special characters which mark off the human world from the animal. Marx's view of Darwin's work led him to express scornful criticisms of those who attempted to apply evolutionary theory to the study of social relations. Reference has already been made to the way in which Marx, in order to gain an audience for his book, instructed Engels to hoodwink Karl Mayer, the editor of *Der Beobachter*. In a letter to Dr. Kugelmann of 6 March 1868, only three months after he had underlined the similarity between Darwin and himself for the review of *Capital* in *Der Beobachter,* Marx made it clear that his method was, in fact, derived from Hegel's dialectic: "Hegel's dialectic is the basic form of all dialectic, but only after it has been stripped of its mystical form, and it is precisely this which distinguishes my method."

In another letter to Kugelmann on 5 December 1868, Marx made caustic remarks about Ludwig Buchner's Lectures on Darwinism saying that "the superficial nonsense about the history of materialism is obviously copied from Lange". In 1870 Marx directed similar invective against a book by F.A. Lange - who was much admired among the German workers and impressed August Bebel - in which Lange tried to interpret social struggles in evolutionary terms as a "struggle for life": "Herr Lange", said Marx, "has made a great discovery. The whole of history can be brought under a single great natural law. This natural law is the *phrase* (in this application Darwin's expression becomes nothing but a phrase) 'the struggle for life', and the content of this phrase is the Malthusian law of population or, rather, over-population. So, instead of analysing the struggle for life as represented historically in varying and definite forms of society, all that has to be done is to translate every concrete struggle into the phrase, 'struggle for life', and this phrase itself into the Malthusian population fantasy. One must admit that this is a very impressive method - for swaggering, sham-scientific, bombastic ignorance and intellectual laziness."[36] In a letter to Laura and Paul Lafargue (15 February, 1869), Marx, signing himself "Old Nick", wrote: "Recognition of the struggle for existence in English society - the war of all against all, bellum omnium contra omnes - led Darwin to discover the struggle for survival as the dominating law of animal and plant life. Darwinism, on the contrary, considers this to be a decisive reason for human society never attaining emancipation from its animal essence."[37]

Marx himself (sometimes aided by Engels) referred to "different races and nationalities, of which it is hard to say which is the least fit for progress and civilisation", to "the physical and intellectual power of the German nation to subdue, absorb, and assimilate its ancient eastern neighbours", to "The classes and the races, too weak to master the new conditions of life, [which] must give way". And, in words described by Bernard Semmel as "Social Darwinism in Marxist vestments", Marx declared: "Such is the redeeming feature of war; it puts a nation to the test. As exposure to the atmosphere reduces all mummies to instant dissolution, so war passes supreme judgement upon social organisations that have outlived their vitality."[38]

4. Dialectics or Science?

As already shown, Marx (in his *Theories of Surplus Value* and elsewhere) utilised a refashioning of the dialectic of Hegel to project a view of history in which individuals and whole classes are sacrificed in a process which, he declared, would necessarily lead humanity to communist society. When Marx wrote in August 1866 (in the first of his letters about Trémaux) that "Progress, which is pure chance with Darwin, is here a necessity ...", he was saying exactly what Herbert Spencer had said over fifteen years earlier in his *Social Statics* (1851): "Progress, therefore, is not an accident, but a necessity." This process of adaptation until man becomes perfect was for Spencer "the realization of the Divine Idea". Spencer's outlook was teleological and his approach was like that of Marx in that "he did not start off from a phenomenon to be explained, but from ethical and metaphysical positions to be established". Darwin, however, went out of his way to make it plain that "progress is no invariable rule". (*The Descent of Man,* Part 1, Chap. V).[39]

On 12 November, 1875, in a letter to Peter Lavrov, echoing Marx's letters of 18 June, 1862 and 15 February 1869, Engels wrote: "The whole Darwinian theory of the struggle for existence is simply the transference from society to animate nature of Hobbes's theory of the war of every man against every man and the bourgeois economic theory of competititon, along with the Malthusian theory of population. This feat having been accomplished - (as indicated under (1) I dispute its unqualified justification, especially where the Malthusian theory is concerned) - the same theories are next transferred back again from organic nature to history and their validity as eternal laws of human society declared to have been proved."[40]This passage also appears, virtually verbatim, in Engels's *Dialectics of Nature* (apparently written between 1873 and 1886). Such views have been repeated, more recently, by S. Timpanaro (*On Materialism*) and in an essay by Ted Benton (in *Issues In Marxist Philosophy*, Vol. 2: Materialism, 1979).

Marx's misinterpretation of Malthus, as stated by Zirkle, and of Hobbes, as indicated by Ferri, has already been noted. "To conclude, as Harris has done, that Darwin's theory of evolution by natural selection is an ideological 'product' of 'early industrial capitalism',[41] stemming not from his scientific enquiries, but from Malthusian doctrine alone, is", says the anthropologist Derek Freeman, "to distort the facts of history ... such specious interpretations will be seen for what they are by all knowledgeable students of the history of evolutionary biology."[42] The genesis of Darwin's theory of the origin of species may be traced, says Freeman, to March 1837, eighteen months before Darwin read Malthus in September 1838. Darwin's discovery was made on the basis of the extensive *prior* development of his specifically scientific enquiries, aided by the stimulus given to his thinking by his reading of Malthus. Darwin's voyage round the world as a naturalist on H.M.S. *Beagle,* from December 1831 to October 1836, afforded him exceptional opportunities to investigate a wide range of biological, geological, and related natural phenomena. And, as Darwin says in his *Autobiography,* when he read Malthus he was already "well prepared to appreciate the struggle for existence which everywhere goes on, from long-continued observation of the habits of animals and plants, ...". "It was in the writings of Lyell [i.e. Charles Lyell, author of *Principles of Geology*] that Darwin first encountered the concept of struggle for existence, not in Malthus", declares Ernst Mayr.[43] Nor did Darwin, says Mayr, get his concept of selection from

Malthus. As Darwin himself stated repeatedly, he got it from the animal breeders.

Darwin's own application of his theory to the investigation of the origin of human society in his book *The Descent of Man and Selection in Relation to Sex* was published in 1871. There is, however, only one reference to Darwin in Marx's ethnological notebooks, and in a letter to Karl Kautsky (16 February, 1884), cited by Diane Paul (op.cit., p. 125), Engels wrote: "On the original states of society there is a *definitive* book, a book as definitive as Darwin's for biology: it has, of course, been discovered by Marx: Morgan, *Ancient Society,* 1877."[44] When writing *Origin of the Family, Private Property and the State* in 1884, Engels used Morgan's work and notes made by Marx as his starting-point. But it is worth noting, as both Marvin Harris and Diane Paul have pointed out, that Morgan - who, said Engels, "rediscovered afresh in America, in his own way, the materialist conception of history" - was, in regard to blacks, an extreme racist. Morgan believed the black race to be so backward as to seem to refute the evidence for the common origin of all human races. In *Systems of Consanguinity and Affinity,* a book familiar to both Marx and Engels, he characterized blacks as "Unimportant in numbers, feeble in intellect, and inferior in rank to every other portion of the human family, ... They seem to challenge and to traverse all the evidences of the unity of origin of the human family ... In the light of our present knowledge the negro is the chief stumbling block in the way of establishing the unity of origin of the human family, upon the basis of scientific proofs." And on another occasion, as quoted by Harris, Morgan said of blacks: "It is too thin a race intellectually to be fit to propagate and I am perfectly satisfied from reflection that the feeling towards this race is one of hostility throughout the north. We have no respect for them whatever." (Cited by Diane Paul, op.cit., pp. 125-26).[45]

Darwin said of man: "That he is capable of incomparably greater and more rapid improvement than is any other animal, admits of no dispute; and this is mainly due to his power of speaking and handing down his acquired knowledge. ... But development of all kinds depends on many concurrent favourable circumstances. Natural selection acts only tentatively. ... With highly civilized nations continued progress depends in a subordinate degree on natural selection; ... Important as the struggle for existence has been and even still is, yet as far as the highest part of man's nature is concerned there are other agencies more important." On the other hand, "Man, like every other animal, has no doubt advanced to his present high condition through a struggle for existence consequent on his rapid multiplication; and if he is to advance still higher, it is to be feared that he must remain subject to a severe struggle." Thus Darwin attempted to balance the influence of cultural factors in social evolution against the effects of natural selection in the struggle for existence. Contemplating the decline of the Greek and Spanish civilizations, Darwin concluded that such retrogression "has too often occurred in the history of the world. We must remember that progress is no invariable rule."[46]

In May 1876, an uprising of the Bulgarians in their struggle for liberation from Turkish rule was harshly repressed by the Turks and, say D. Djordjevic and S. Fischer-Galati,[47] "30,000 people died either in battle or at the hand of Turkish authorities." These atrocities evoked a great outburst of anti-Turkish feeling in England. In a letter to Engels dated 11 December 1876,[48] Marx criticised Darwin for publicly supporting the Conference on the Eastern Question which had been held in London on 8 December 1876. The Conference supported the Bulgarian victims of Turkish oppression and urged England to join with Russia to force Turkey to make reforms. Darwin gave several donations to the Bulgarians and supported Russia. Marx however, was pro-Turk. He hated and feared Russia and had ranged himself on the side of Turkey during the Crimean War. Both he and Engels also gave full support to the Turks in the Russo-Turkish war. On 4 February, 1878, Marx sent to Wilhelm Liebknecht, who was a member of the German Reichstag, a letter of advice on the war, proclaiming the virtues of the Turks. Marx wrote: "We are decidedly in favour of the Turks ... we have studied the Turkish peasant i.e. the mass of the Turkish people, and found him undoubtedly one of the most capable and morally upright representatives of the European peasantry, ...".[49] These "morally upright" Turks had, in fact, perpetrated hideous massacres which had aroused such a strong revulsion of feeling in 1876. From 1894 to 1915 these "most moral" fellows would carry out one massacre after another, of the most brutal character. The Turks were aiming at the extermination of the entire Armenian race. Probably about 800,000 people died as a result.[50] According to Nathaniel Weyl, "Hitler's study of the successful annihilation of the Armenians by the Turkish and Kurdish peasantry helped convince him that the destruction of European Jewry was practicable." (op.cit., p.129).

In what has been called "the standard English biography of Marx", David McLellan says that the view of Marx and Darwin expressed by Engels in his speech at Marx's graveside "is highly misleading". And in a recent account of Darwin, Jonathan Howard refers to the "incredible heterogeneity of philosophical ideals that have used the Darwinian theory of evolution as a justifying principle." Whereas Alfred Schmidt contends that "... Marx accepted no rigid facts about man", in Perry D. Westbrook's view, Darwin's basic theory "is less rigid than that of Marx. Darwin cannot admit of an ineluctable determinism working towards certain ends...".[51]

In his Afterword of 24 January 1873 to the Second German Edition of Volume 1 of *Capital*, Marx quoted approvingly from an article published in 1872 in St. Petersburg describing the dialectical method he employed in his book: "Marx treats the social movement as a process of natural history, governed by laws not only independent of human will, consciousness and intelligence, but rather, on the contrary, determining that will, consciousness and intelligence... If in the history of civilisation the conscious element plays a part so subordinate, then it is self-evident that a critical inquiry whose subject matter is civilisation, can, less than anything else, have for its basis any form of, or any result of, consciousness." Lenin, in his *What The "Friends of the People" Are* (p. 58) comments that, as Marx himself says, this description of the method of *Capital* is "absolutely correct". Lenin goes on to quote Marx's dictum that "the ideal is nothing but the reflection of the material" and concludes that "the whole matter thus amounts to an 'affirmative recognition of the existing state of things and of its inevitable development'."[52] The important question today, says Diane Paul, is "to what extent Marxist categories are informed by the nineteenth-century cultural prejudices of Marx and Engels". (op.cit., p.138).

Quoting the opinion of C. Wright Mills that Karl Marx "was *the* social and political thinker of the nineteenth century," Marvin Harris adds: "It remains to be shown, however, that this eminence adds up to a scientific contribution analogous to that which is generally attributed to Darwin. ... The Marxist stress on the unity of theory and practice contains an implicit threat to the most fundamental rule of the

scientific method, namely, the obligation to report data honestly. ...
Spencer's fetishistic veneration of competition as expressed in the
phrase 'survival of the fittest', has its counterpart in Marx's Hegelian
infatuation with 'contradictions'."[53] Elsewhere, Harris writes: "two
defects in Marx's formulation must be noted: First, Marx argued for
the imminence of radical sociocultural change on the basis of and in
conformity with Hegel's notion of dialectics. Orthodox Marxism has
never recovered from this crippling heritage. Second, Marx's initial
formulations were made without benefit of a knowledge of prehistory
or primitive cultures and reflected Hegel's contempt for peoples
whom the world-spirit had ignored or left behind."[54]

Peter Singer's assessment, in his clear and succinct study,[55] is that
Marx's main theoretical achievements "are not scientific discoveries"
as Engels and others claimed. Marx's view of society is illuminating,
but it does not amount to a scientific discovery of "the law of
development of human history" comparable to Darwin's theory of
evolution.

NOTES

1. Stephen Jay Gould and Niles Eldredge, "Punctuated Equilibria:
the Tempo and Mode of Evolution Reconsidered", *Paleobiology*,
1977, Vol. 3; Richard Lewontin, Steven Rose, and Leo Kamin, *Race
and Class*, Summer, 1982 - extract from *Not In Our Genes: biology,
ideology and human nature*, to be published in 1983.

2. Lewis S. Feuer, "Is the 'Darwin-Marx Correspondence'
Authentic?", *Annals of Science* 32 (Jan. 1975), and "The Case of the
'Darwin-Marx' Letter", *Encounter*, October 1978. Also, Margaret
A. Fay, "Marx and Darwin", *Monthly Review*, March 1980, and
Ralph Colp, Jr. "The Myth of the Darwin-Marx Letter", *History of
Political Economy* 14:4 (1982). See, further, Terence Ball, "Marx
and Darwin - A Reconsideration", *Political Theory*, November
1979.
In her book, *Biological Politics* (1982, p. 181), Janet Sayers
declares: "Indeed, Marx dedicated a copy of *Capital* to Darwin (Fay,
1980)." The point of Margaret Fay's article in the March, 1980 issue
of *Monthly Review* was, of course, to demonstrate that Marx "never
had any intention of dedicating any of his work to Darwin. ... Marx's
offer to dedicate any of his work to Darwin was finally revealed for

138

what it really is: a myth ...". (Fay, 1980, pp.53-4, 56).

3. Conway Zirkle, *Evolution, Marxian Biology and the Social Scene,* 1959.

4. Shlomo Avineri, "From Hoax to Dogma", *Encounter,* March, 1967.

5. V.I. Lenin, *What The "Friends of the People" Are,* Moscow, 1970, p.21.

6. G. Plekhanov, *The Development of the Monist View of History.*

7. Marx to Kugelmann, 11 October, 1867.

8. See Igor Shafarevich, *The Socialist Phenomenon* (1980), pp. 267-68. Also Leopold Schwarzschild, *The Red Prussian* (1948), pp. 291-92. These letters may be found in Marx-Engels, *Werke,* Vols. 31 and 32 (1965).

9. Enrique M. Ureña, "Marx and Darwin", *History of Political Economy,* 9:4 (1977); Marx-Engels, *Werke,* Vol. 31.

10. Avineri, op. cit; Lewis S. Feuer, "Marx and Engels as Sociobiologists", *Survey,* Autumn (1977-78); Marx-Engels, *Werke,* Vol. 31.

11. Shafarevich, op. cit., pp. 211-12; David McLellan, *Engels* (1977), pp. 72-73. Daniel Gasman refers to "The attempt on the part of the Marxists to share in the prestige of Darwinism and bolster their own position by attaching themselves to it...". (*The Scientific Origins of National Socialism,* 1971, p.111).

12. V. Gerratana, "Marx and Darwin", *New Left Review* (1973).

13. Grace Carlton, *Friedrich Engels, the Shadow Prophet* (1965). p.43.

14. As to when Marx became a communist, see David McLellan, *Marxism Before Marx,* Second Edition, 1980, p. 184.

Regarding the influence on Marx of German philosophers, particularly

Hegel, Engels states: "Without German philosophy, particularly that of Hegel, German scientific socialism (the only scientific Socialism extant) would never have come into existence". (*The Peasant War in Germany,* Third authorised edition, 1875, Addendum to Preface. Translated 1927, p.27).

15. "Marx himself was committed to a specific goal of human history - communism - and a specific role for the proletariat *before* he developed the historical analysis which, as he believed, demonstrated its ineluctability. Indeed before he knew very much about the proletariat." Eric Hobsbawm, "Looking Forward: History and the Future", *New Left Review,* Jan.-Feb., 1981.

16. Marx-Engels, *Collected Works,* Vol. 3 (1975), pp.296-97.

17. E. Durkheim, *Selected Writings* (1981) pp. 156-57.

18. James R. Moore, *The Post-Darwinian Controversies* (1979), p.373.

19. *Economic and Philosophical Manuscripts* (1844), [Estranged Labour]; *The Holy Family,* Chap. IV. 4); *Capital,* Volume 1 : Chap. XXIV, Preface to the First German Edition, Chap. XXXII.

20. Allen E. Buchanan, *Marx and Justice,* 1982, pp. 24-25.

21. Z.A. Jordan, *The Evolution of Dialectical Materialism,* 1967, p. 313.

22. Marvin Harris, *Cultural Materialism,* 1979, p.66. See also pp. 150,155.

23. Bober, op. cit., pp. 36, 385,386; see also p. 44.

In a systematic criticism in *New Left Review* (Sept.-Oct. 1980) of G.A. Cohen's book, *Karl Marx's Theory of History: A Defence* (1978), Andrew Levine and Erik Olin Wright conclude that the theory of socialist revolution cannot be derived from an account of the fettering of the development of the forces of production: "The 'orthodoxy' Cohen has reconstructed and defended is, in our view, ultimately inadequate politically, as well as theoretically, whatever its roots in Marx's writings."

24. For further discussion, see Zirkle, op.cit., and Introduction by Antony Flew to Malthus, *On the Principle of Population,* Pelican Books, 1970, Reprinted 1979.

25. V.L. Komarov, "Marx and Engels on Biology", in N.I. Bukharin et al., *Marxism and Modern Thought,* 1935.

26. In *Darwin and Modern Science, Essays in Commemoration of the Centenary of the Birth of Charles Darwin ...,* Edited by A.C. Seward, 1909, p. 474.

27. Enrico Ferri, *Socialism and Positive Science (Darwin-Spencer-Marx),* 1905 (originally, 1894).

28. Marx, *Theories of Surplus Value,* Part II, [Chap. IX], Section [2.

29. In a letter to Joseph Weydemeyer (5 March, 1852), Marx wrote: "What I did that was new was to prove: ... (2) that the class struggle necessarily leads to the dictatorship of the proletariat; and (3) that this dictatorship itself only constitutes the transition to the abolition of all classes and to a classless society."

30. Pierre Trémaux, "Origines et transformations de l'homme et des autres êtres. Première partie," Paris, 1865. The letters of Marx and Engels relating to Trémaux are quoted and discussed by Zirkle, op.cit.; Feuer, "Marx and Engels as Sociobiologists"; Nathaniel Weyl, *Karl Marx: Racist,* 1979; Diane Paul, " 'In the Interests of Civilization': Marxist Views of Race and Culture in the Nineteenth Century", *Journal of the History of Ideas,* Jan.-March, 1981. Translations from two of the letters written by Marx are also in *The Letters of Karl Marx: Selected and Translated with Explanatory Notes and an Introduction* by Saul K. Padover, New Jersey, 1979.

31. Marvin Harris (*The Rise of Anthropological Theory,* 1969) quotes Zirkle (1959) but not Zirkle's account of the correspondence between Marx and Engels about Trémaux.

Komarov ("Marx and Engels on Biology", 1935) paraphrases Marx's letter to Engels of 7 August 1866 but omits any reference to Marx's endorsement of Trémaux's assertion that Negroes had degenerated from a much higher type.

32. Edmund Silberner, "Was Marx an anti-Semite?"; C. Zirkle, *Evolution, Marxian Biology, and the Social Scene;* Carlos Moore, *Were Marx and Engels White Racists?;* W.H. Chaloner and W.O. Henderson, "Marx/Engels and Racism"; N.Weyl, *Karl Marx: Racist.*

33. John C. Greene, "Darwin as a Social Evolutionist", *Journal of the History of Biology,* Vol. 10, no. 1 (Spring 1977).

S. Timpanaro says that "Darwinism by destroying the notion of the fixity of species and thereby establishing a genetic affinity between the various human races or species, dealt a serious blow to racism, ...". (*On Materialism,* 1980, p.49, Note 21).

34. James R. Moore, *The Post-Darwinian Controversies,* 1979, pp.316-17.

35. Marx-Engels, *Collected Works,* Vol. 38 (1982), pp. 102, 103.

36. Marx, *Letters to Dr. Kugelmann,* 1941, pp. 63, 80, 111.

Gasman (op.cit. pp. xiii, xxiii) says that "Darwinism in Germany was a system of thought that was often transformed almost beyond recognition. *Darwinismus* was far from the biological ideas or underlying moral and philosophical views of Darwin himself." ... racially inspired social Darwinism in Germany, which was almost completely indebted to Haeckel for its creation, [and which] on the whole had little, if anything at all, to do with Charles Darwin, ...". Diane Paul (op.cit. p. 126) comments: "Haeckel's views had come to be so closely associated with racism that it might be expected that Engels at least (since he was far more concerned with Haeckel than was Marx) would separate himself from that aspect of his [Haeckel's] theory, ...".

37. Marx-Engels, *Werke,* Vol. 32 (1965), p.592.

38. Marx-Engels, *Collected Works,* Vol. 12, p. 7; Vol. 11, p. 71; Vol. 11, p.531; Vol. 14, p.516.

Bernard Semmel, Introduction to *Marxism and the Science of War,* 1981.

It may be added that Engels, in articles in the *Neue Rheinische Zeitung,* declared that:... "the Austrian Germans and Magyars will be set free and wreak a bloody revenge on the Slav barbarians. The general war which will then break out will smash this Slav league and wipe out all these petty, hidebound nations down to their very names. The next world war will result in the disappearance from the face of the earth not only of reactionary classes and dynasties, but also of entire reactionary peoples. And that, too, is a step forward. ... only by the most determined use of terror against these Slav peoples can we, jointly with the Poles and Magyars, safeguard the revolution." Marx-Engels, *Collected Works,* Vol. 8, pp. 238,378.

As Engels subsequently stated: "The editorial constitution" of the *Neue Rheinische Zeitung* "was simply the dictatorship of Marx". (Marx-Engels, *Selected Works,* Moscow, 1958, Vol. II, p. 300).

There is a very useful, concise collection of little known writings of Marx and Engels on Race, Nationalities, Colonialism, and War, 1844-1894: *What Marx and Engels Said About the Slavs - Irish - Jews - Blacks - and Others* (see reference in *The Guardian* Diary, March 29, 1983). The third (1987) edition of this collection, assembled by me, is at Appendix I to the present volume.

39. For Spencer, see J.D.Y. Peel, *Herbert Spencer,* 1971, pp. 101, 132, 215. "Darwin's rejection of the doctrine of necessary progress was in marked opposition to many of the biologists of his day", says Derek Freeman (see Note 42).

40. See Ronald L. Meek, *Marx and Engels on Malthus,* 1953, p. 176.

41. Krader, also, has written: "The social doctrine of unbridled individualism in Hobbes is actually descriptive of the relations of civil society, as Hegel recognized it to be. Darwin then spiritualized the animal kingdom, or the of kingdom of nature generally, in order that it be made to figure as civil society." *The Ethnological Notebooks of Karl Marx,* p. 393, Note 157.

But Krader fails to supply any concrete evidence whatsoever for these assertions.

42. Derek Freeman, "The Evolutionary Theories of Charles Darwin and Herbert Spencer", with fifteen commentaries and a reply by Freeman. *Current Anthropology,* Vol. 15, No. 3, September, 1974.

43. Ernst Mayr, *The Growth of Biological Thought,* 1982, p. 483.

See also Dominique Lecourt, *Proletarian Science? The Case of Lysenko*, 1977, pp. 92-93.

44. In the Soviet English-language edition of the *Selected Correspondence* of Marx and Engels (Third Revised Edition, 1975), the word "important" is used in place of "definitive" in this sentence. But none of the dictionaries that have been consulted gives the meaning "important" for the German word "entscheidend" (*Werke*, Vol. 36 (1967), p. 109) which is construed as "decisive, definitive".

45. Morgan also wrote, in *Ancient Society*, of "the plan of the Supreme Intelligence to develop a barbarian out of a savage, and a civilized man out of this barbarian."

In a discussion of Morgan's work in *Current Anthropology*, Morris E. Opler says: "Whether or not they [Marx and Engels] misread him [Morgan], they most certainly misrepresented him." (Vol. 5 No. 2, April 1964, p. 111). Morgan, says Marvin Harris, "was a typical Spencerian with strong idealist commitments". (Ibid., Vol. 9 No. 5, December 1968, p. 520).

46. C. Darwin, *The Descent of Man*, Part 1, Chaps. III and V; Part II, Chap. XXI.

Brian Easlea talks about "Darwin's two souls" (*Science and Sexual Oppression*, 1981, pp. 154-57).

But Khrushchev took a more down-to-earth view. He was fond of saying, write F.S. Northedge and Audrey Wells, that "The West and the Soviet Union are like animals in Noah's ark: they can only protect themselves against the nothingness outside by accepting the fact that each will fight for its life if it thinks its existence is threatened, but that in respect for each other's existence lies the most effective guarantee of its own". (Northedge and Wells, *Britain and Soviet Communism*, 1982, pp. 247-48).

47. D. Djordjevic and S. Fischer-Galati, *The Balkan Revolutionary Tradition*, 1981, pp. 153-54.

48. See Colp, "The Myth of the Darwin-Marx Letter", pp. 468-69. Marx-Engels, *Werke*, Vol. 34 (1966), p. 28.

49. Quoted by Franz Mehring, *Karl Marx: The Story of His Life*,

Reprinted 1981, p.517. Marx-Engels, *Werke,* Vol. 34.

50. Everyman's Encyclopaedia, Sixth Edition in Twelve Volumes, Volume 1, 1978, pp. 440-41.

51. David McLellan, *Karl Marx: His Life and Thought,* p.424; Jonathan Howard, *Darwin,* 1982, p.90; Alfred Schmidt, *The Concept of Nature in Marx,* 1973, p.48; Perry D. Westbrook, *Free Will and Determinism in American Literature,* 1979, p.100.

52. D.R. Oldroyd in his *Darwinian Impacts,* Open University Press, 1980 (p.242, Note 25), refers to Marx's comments in the Afterword to the second edition of *Capital,* and says "this is not a positive assertion of the doctrine; rather it is an acceptance of it when it is attributed." Later Marxist writers, Oldroyd says, "have tended to repudiate any doctrine of 'historical inevitability'." As an example of what he says is the repudiation of "any doctrine of 'historical inevitability' ", Oldroyd then quotes part of a sentence from a passage, in which Marx's Afterword is not mentioned, in Part 1 of Lenin's *What The "Friends of the People" Are.* But Oldroyd makes no reference to the fact that in the very same Part of the same book, Lenin cites Marx's Afterword and the St. Petersburg article *in extenso,* and repeatedly asserts and justifies the doctrine referred to therein, depicting an "inevitable development". A quotation from page 58 of Lenin's book has already been given. On page 56, after quoting Marx's Afterword, Lenin says it is quite enough if Marx "proves the necessity of another order which must *inevitably* grow out of the preceding one regardless of whether men believe in it or not, whether they are conscious of it or not." On page 72, he refers to "the facts and arguments on which Marx based the conclusion that the socialist system is *inevitable* by virtue of the very laws of capitalist development". On page 73, Lenin says that Marx in his *Capital* "made it his task to give a scientific analysis of the capitalist form of society ... showing that the development of this organisation ... has such and such a tendency, that it must *inevitably* perish and turn into another, a higher organisation". And on page 84, Lenin writes of "Marx's proofs of the *inevitability* of the capitalist system being transformed into a socialist system" (italics added).

53. Marvin Harris, *The Rise of Anthropological Theory,* pp. 218-20, 223. Among his unpublished papers, Engels left a note stating: "The

Darwinian theory to be demonstrated as the practical proof of Hegel's account of the inner connection between necessity and chance". (*Dialectics of Nature*, 1976, p.306). But he evidently never returned to a further discussion of this particular theme. According to Lenin *(One Step Forward, Two Steps Back,* 1904): "oats grow according to Hegel". *(Collected Works,* Moscow, 1965, p.411). As Wilma George says, "No such Hegelian dialectic would be found in Darwinian theory". (*Darwin,* 1982, p.97).

54. *Current Anthropology,* Vol. 9, No. 5, December 1968, pp. 519-20.

55. Peter Singer, Marx, 1980, pp. 40, 67.

C. Leon Harris, *Evolution: Genesis and Revelations,* 1981, is of related interest.

See also, Morris Ginsberg, *Essays in Sociology and Social Philosophy,* Volume Three, Evolution and Progress, 1961, pp. 28-29.

146

NAME INDEX

A

Acton, H.B., 12, 13, 70
Anderson, Perry, 18
Annenkov, P.V., 15, 33, 79, 109
Arvon, Henri, 8, 87
Aveling, Edward B., 49, 119
Avineri, Shlomo, 31, 32, 76, 100, 120, 138

B

Bakunin, M.A., 54-56, 58, 74, 75, 78, 79, 106
Ball, Terence, 137
Barrett, Michèle, 84
Baugh, Graham, 55
Bebel, August, 60, 84, 94, 104, 113, 131
Bell, Daniel, 53
Benn, Tony, 7
Benton, Ted, 133
Bernstein, Eduard, 14
Bienkowski, W., 67
Billig, Michael, 86, 95
Blaug, Mark, 7, 28, 29, 38, 39, 43
Bloch, Maurice, 117
Blumenberg, Werner, 83-84, 94, 95
Bober, M.M., 22, 33, 34-35, 42, 54, 90, 123, 139
Booth, David, 46
Borgius, W., 101
Bottomore, Tom, 72
Boudin, Louis B., 40
Bouglé, C., 125, 131
Buchanan, Allen E., 83, 123, 139

C

Carew-Hunt, R.N., 100

Carey, F.S., 46-48
Carlebach, Julius, 86, 102, 108
Carlton, Grace, 122, 138
Carr, E.H., 54, 82
Carver, Terrell, 36-37, 67, 87, 90-91
Castoriadis, Cornelius, 37, 91
Catephores, George C., 29, 36, 37, 90, 91
Chaloner, W.H., 129, 141
Chandra, Bipan, 30
Chomsky, Noam, 55
Clark, Joseph, 86, 95
Cohen, G.A., 16, 17, 19, 20, 21, 139
Colp Jr., Ralph, 85, 117, 119, 130, 137, 143
Cornforth, Maurice, 120
Cummins, Ian, 25, 81, 89

D

Darwin, Charles, 85, 110, 117-145
Demetz, Peter, 22
Demuth, Hélène, 83
Demuth, Henry Frederick, 83-84
Djordjevic, D., 135, 143
Donald, James, 14
Draper, Hal, 52-53, 85, 86, 93
Duncan, Graeme, 35, 90, 94
Durkheim, Emile, 122, 139

E

Easlea, Brian, 143
Elster, Jon, 28, 53, 56, 91, 94
Engels, Friedrich, 6, 7, 8, 9, 11, 12, 13, 15, 16, 17, 18, 22, 23, 24, 25, 27, 29, 30, 31, 32, 33, 34-35, 36, 42, 44,